The Classical Guitar Collection

50 Favorites by 26 Composers

arrang
Josep

Concert Masterworks

ISBN 978-0-634-04937-8

CREATIVE CONCEPTS PUBLISHING

EXCLUSIVELY DISTRIBUTED BY

HAL•LEONARD® CORPORATION

7777 W. BLUEMOUND RD. P.O. BOX 13819 MILWAUKEE, WI 53213

Visit Hal Leonard Online at
www.halleonard.com

CONTENTS

Romanza

traditional Spanish
folk melody

Air ("On the G String")
from Suite No. 3 for orchestra, BWV 1068

J.S. Bach
(1685-1750)

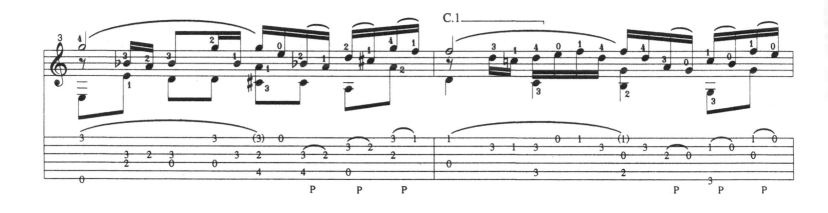

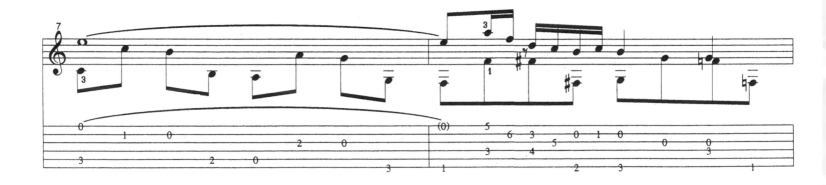

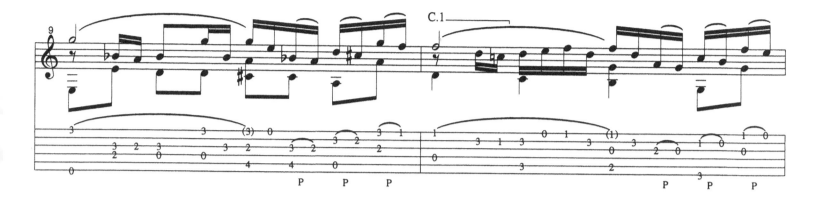

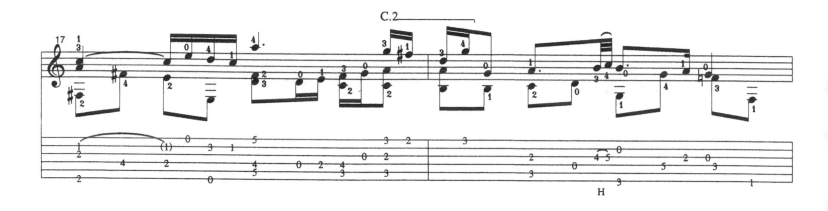

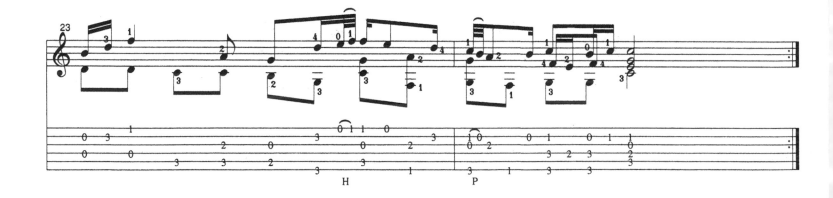

Allemande
from Suite No. 1 for Lute, BWV 996

J.S. Bach
(1685–1750)

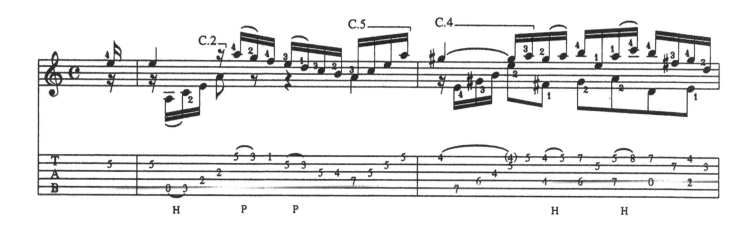

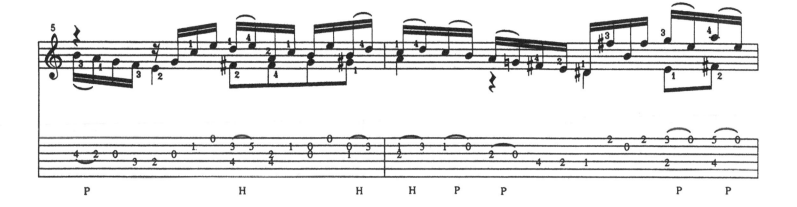

10

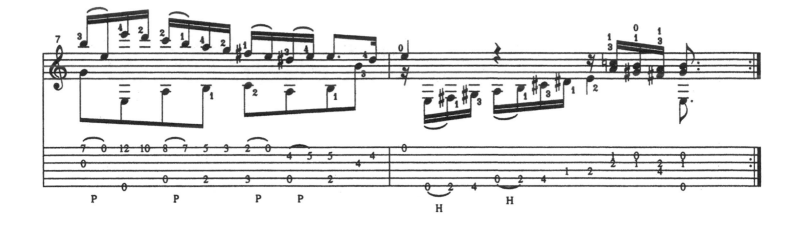

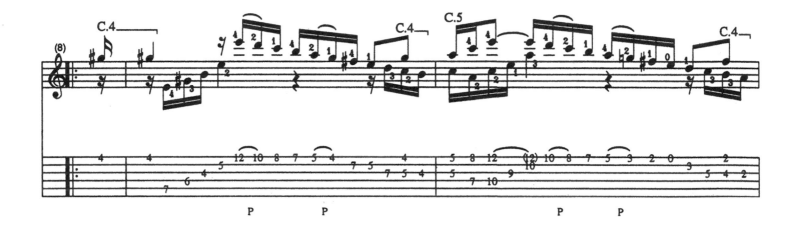

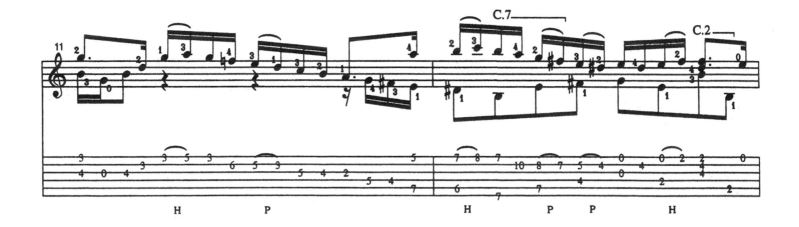

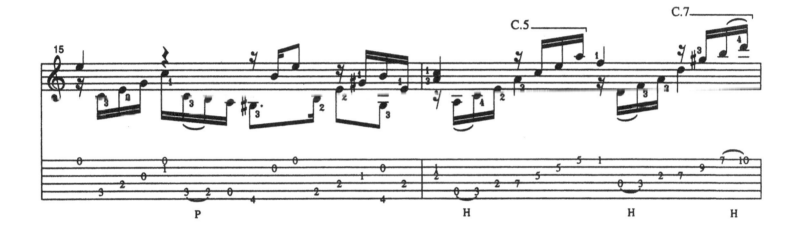

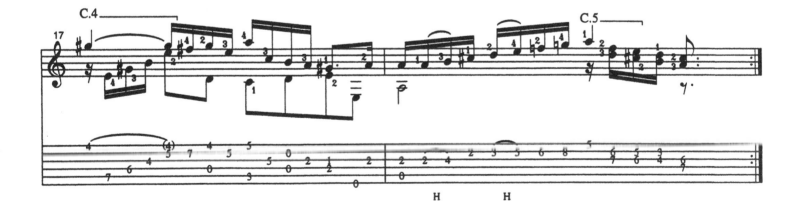

Chorale: "Jesu, Joy of Man's Desiring"
from Cantata No. 147, *"Herz und Mund und Tat und Leben"*

J.S. Bach
(1685-1750)

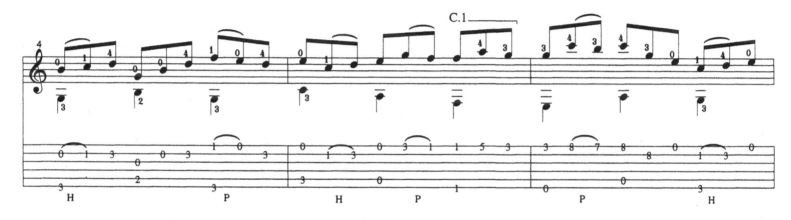

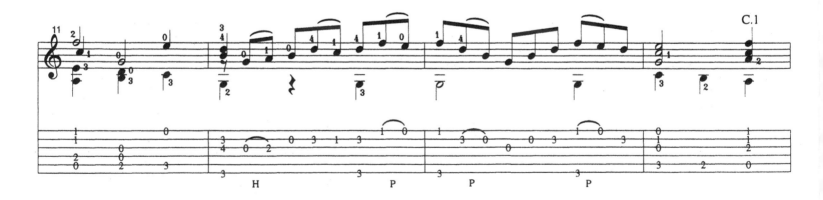

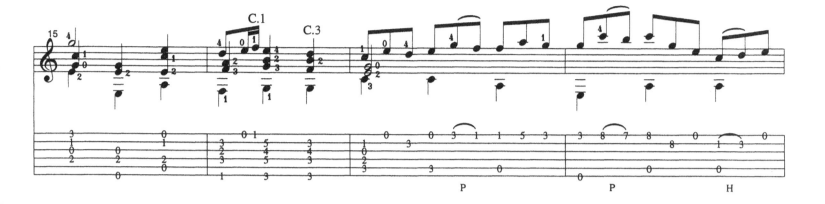

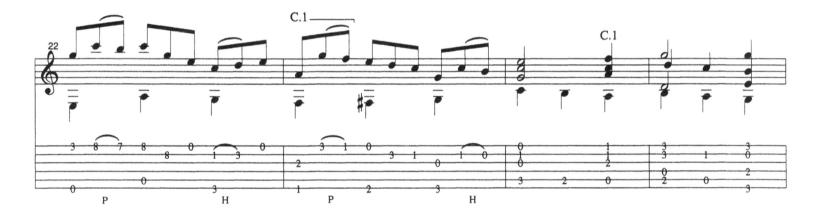

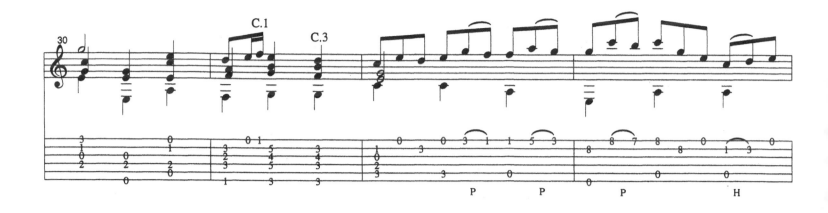

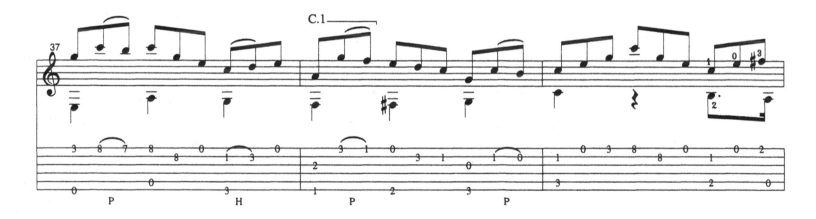

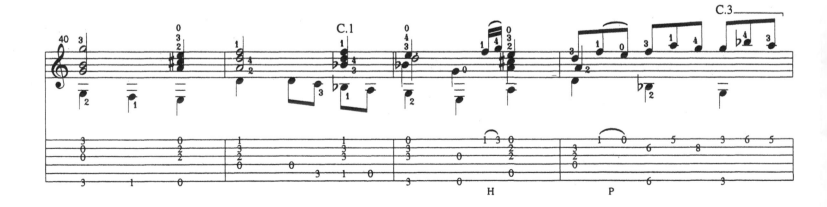

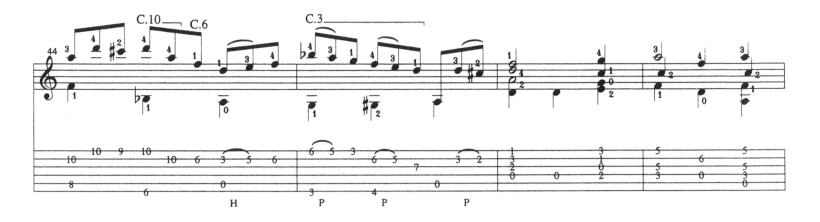

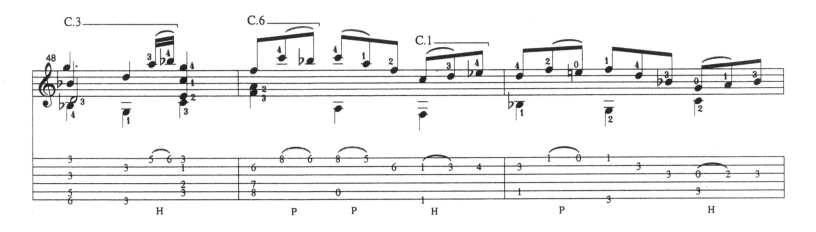

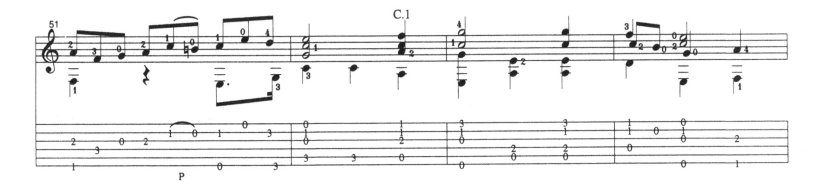

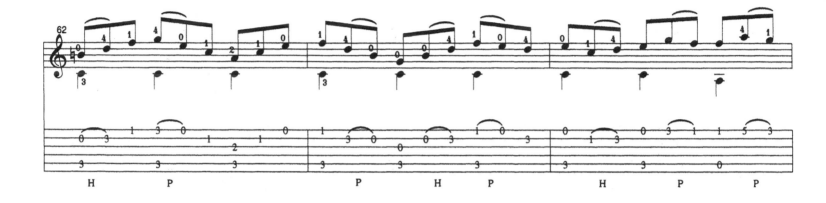

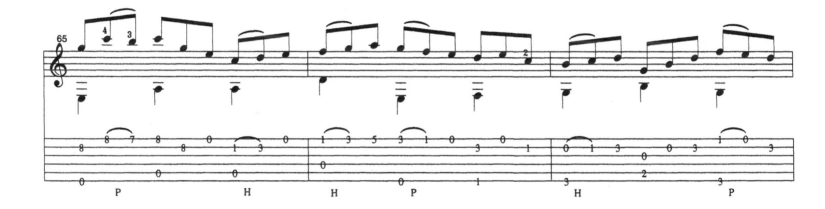

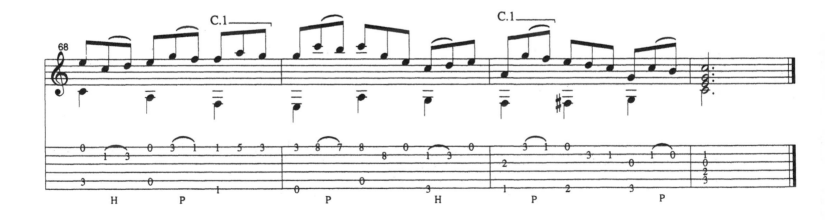

Prelude
from Suite No. 1 for solo cello, BWV 1007

J.S. Bach
(1685-1750)

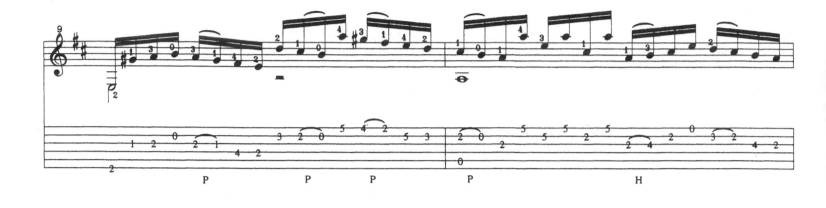

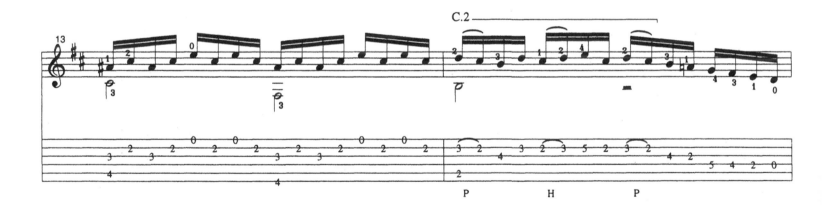

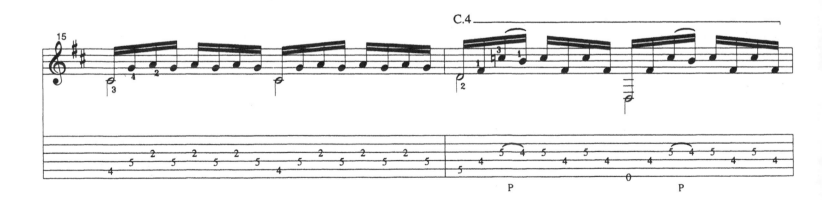

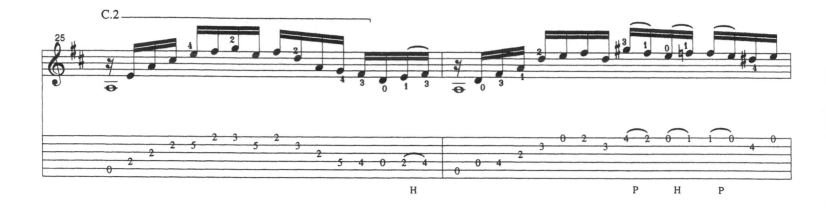

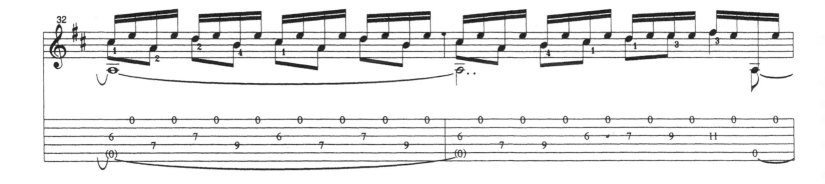

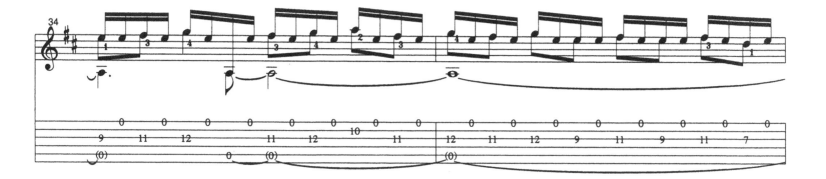

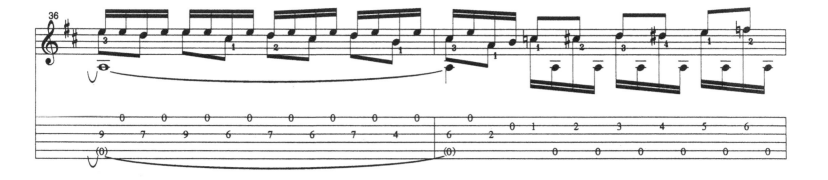

Menuet in G Major

from *Klavierbüchlein für Anna Magdalena Bach* (1725)

J.S. Bach
(1685–1750)

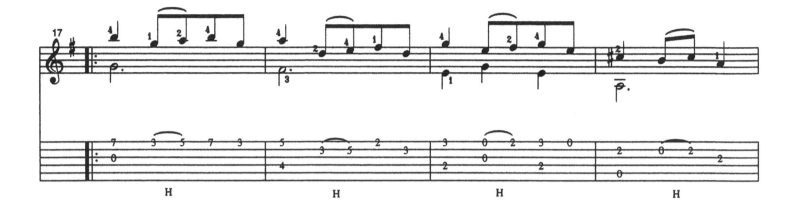

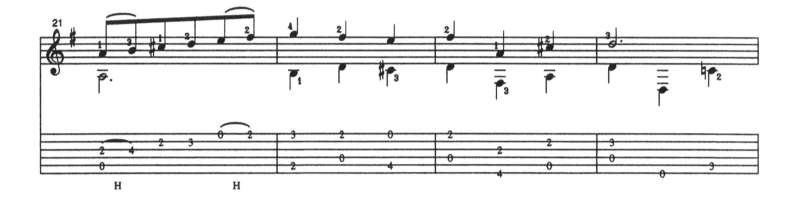

Menuet in G Minor

from *Klavierbüchlein für Anna Magdalena Bach* (1725)

J.S. Bach
(1685–1750)

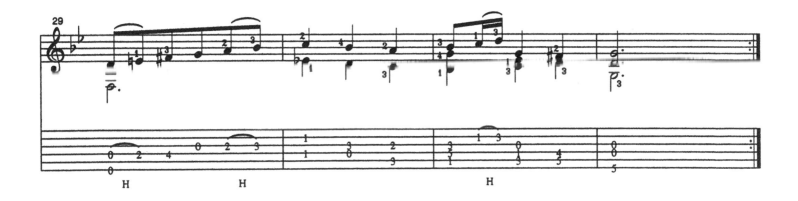

Prelude
for lute, BWV 999

J.S. Bach
(1685-1750)

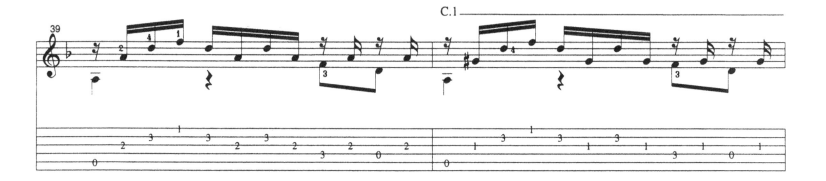

Sarabande
from French Suite No. 1 for keyboard, BWV 812

J.S. Bach
(1685-1750)

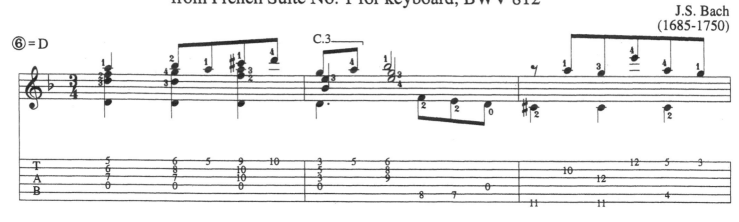

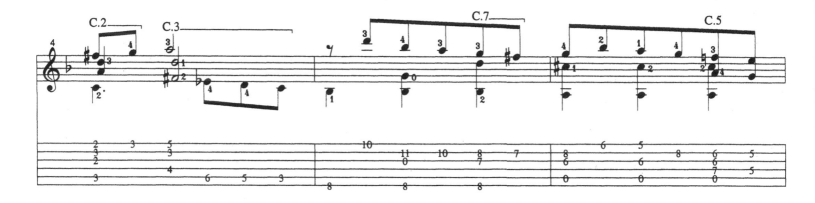

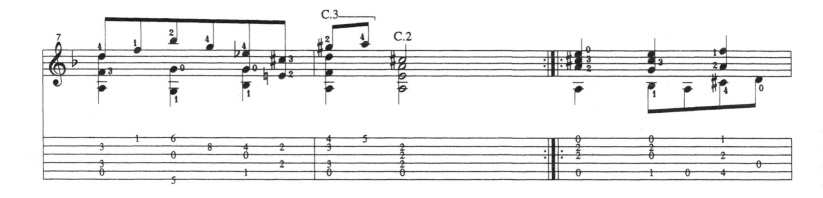

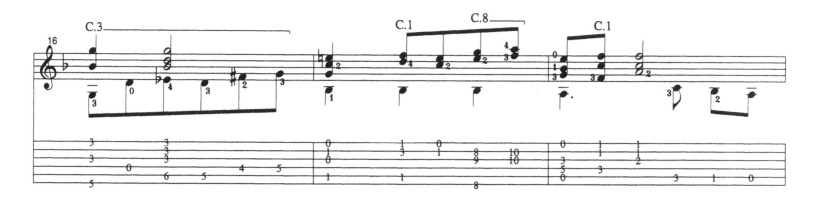

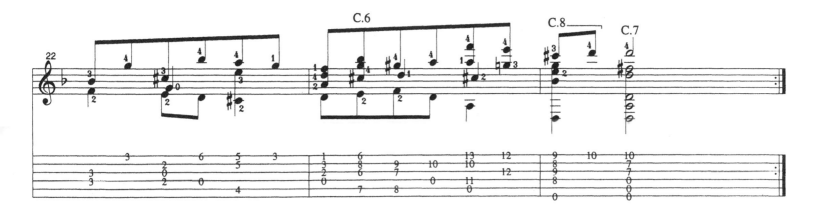

Siciliana
from Sonata No. 1 for solo violin, BWV1001

J.S. Bach
(1685-1750)

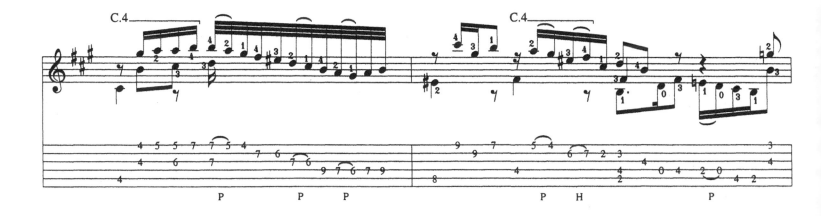

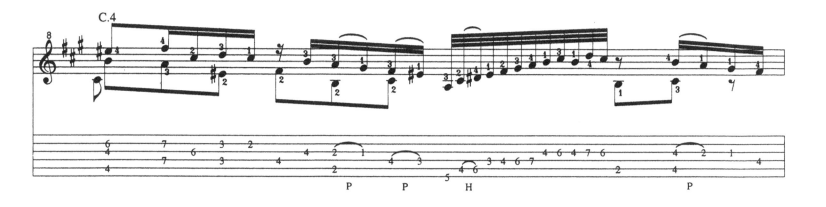

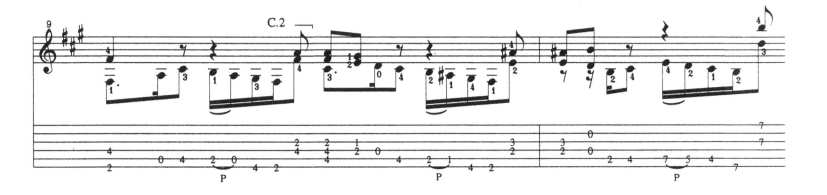

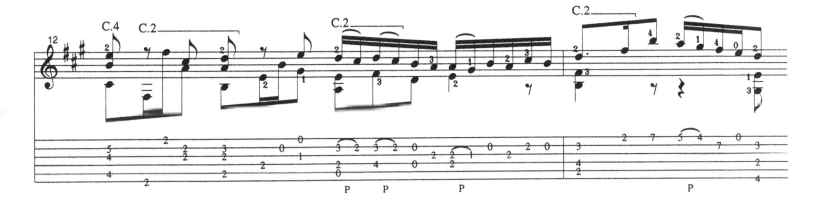

Andantino in C Major

from *Méthode complète pour la guitarre* (1840)

Matteo Carcassi
(1792–1853)

Gavotte en rondeau

Jean François Dandrieu
(1682-1738)

⑥ = D

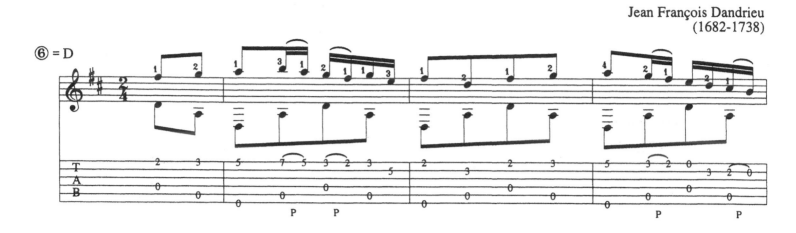

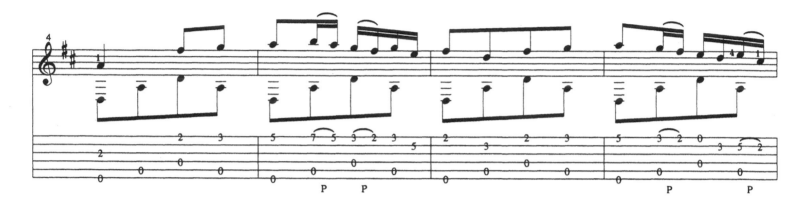

1er Couplet

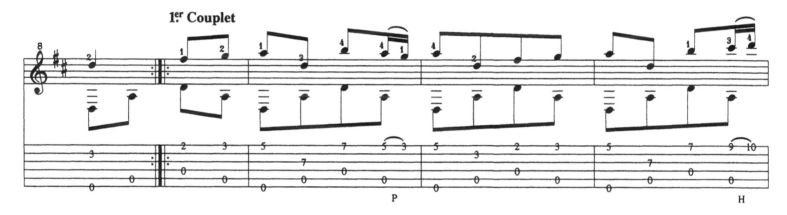

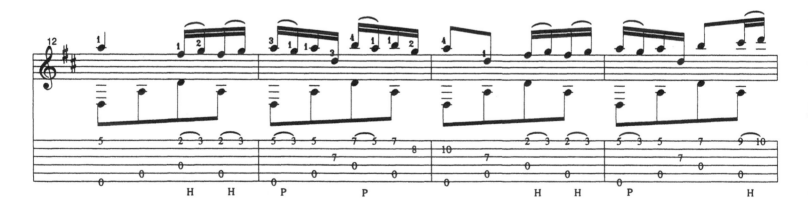

2.ᵉ Couplet

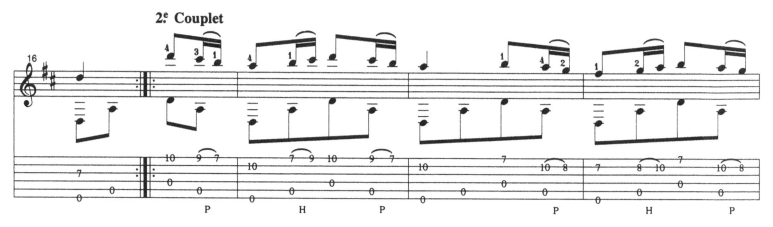

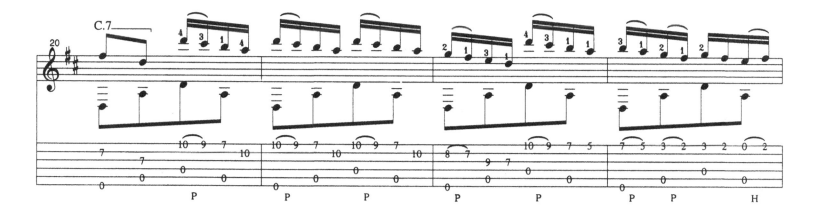

Tarantelle
from *25 Etudes de Genre*, Op. 38

Napoléan Coste
(1806–1883)

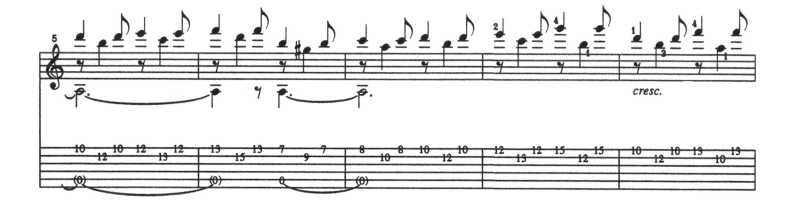

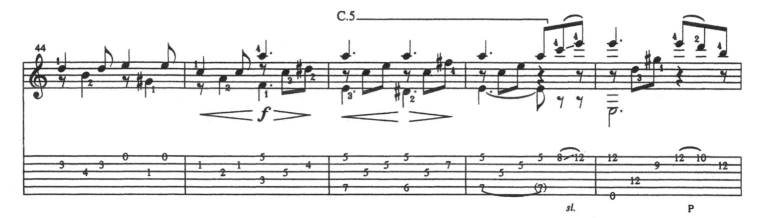

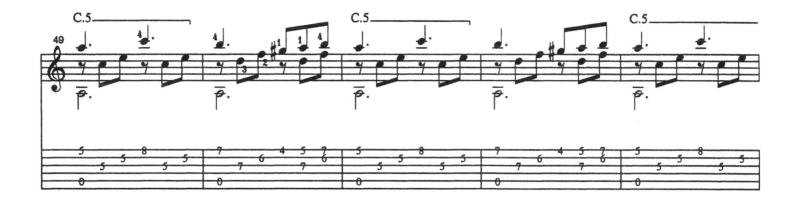

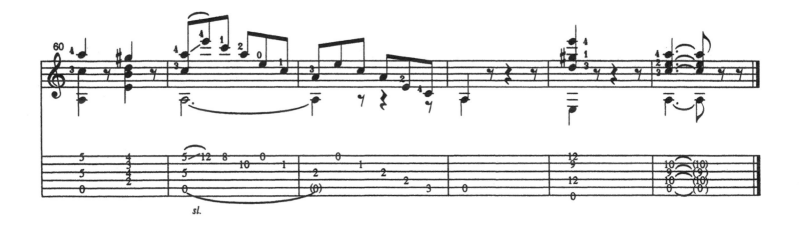

Canción Triste
from *Preludios Vascos*, Book I (1912)

P. José Antonio de Donostía
(1886-1957)

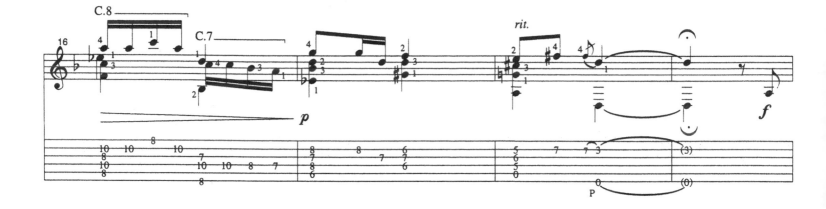

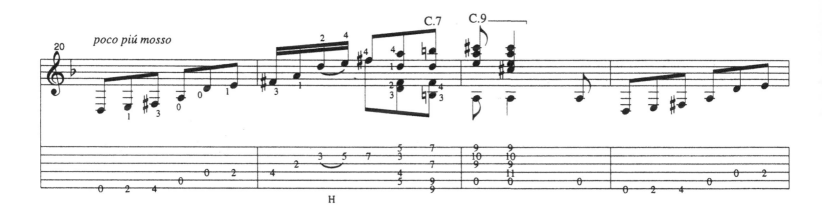

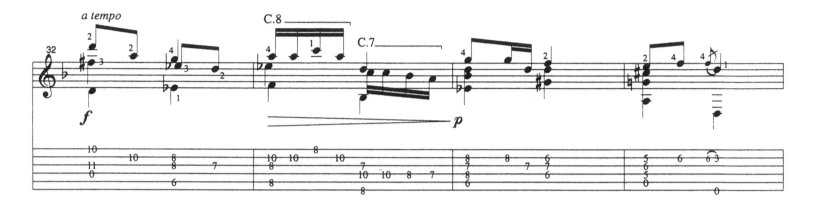

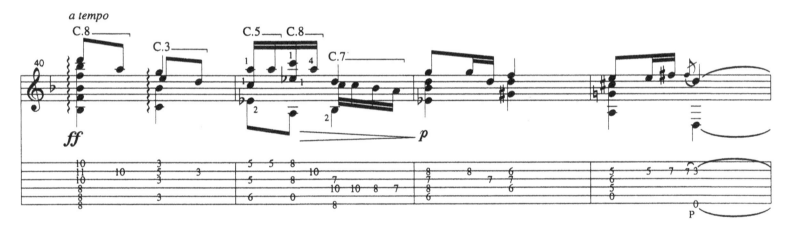

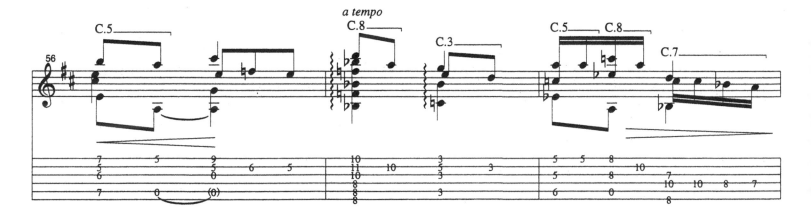

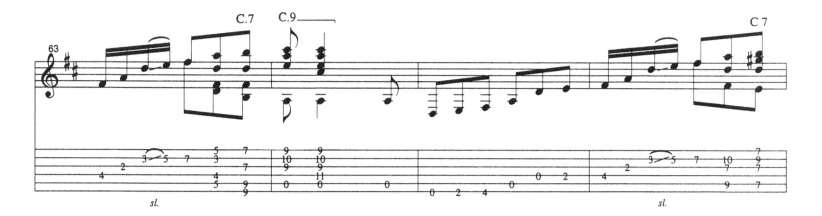

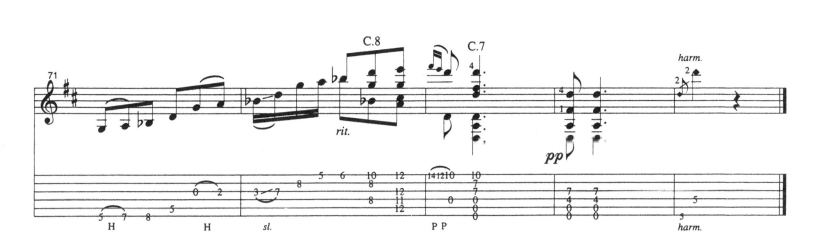

Dolor

from *Preludios Vascos,* Book II (1914)

P. José Antonio de Donostía
(1886-1957)

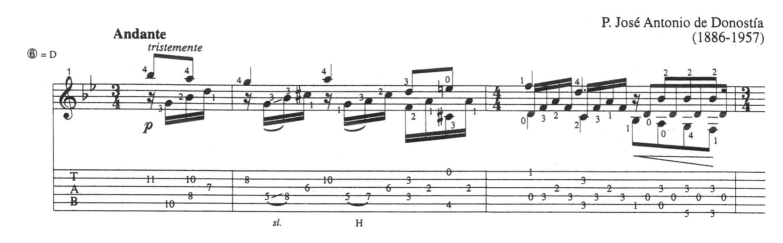

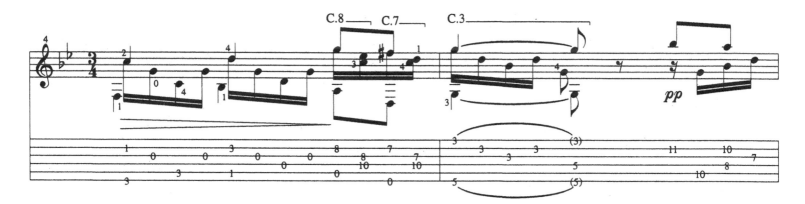

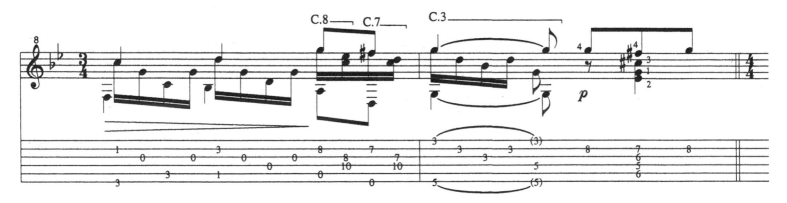

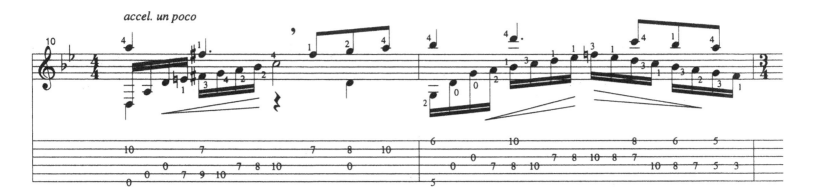

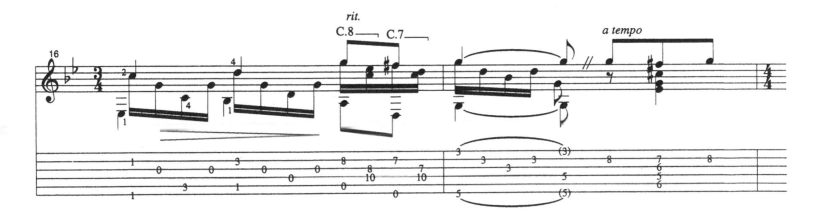

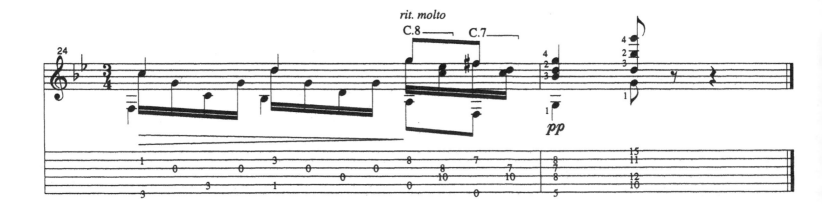

Homenaje
Pour le tombeau de Claude Debussy

Manuel de Falla
(1876-1946)

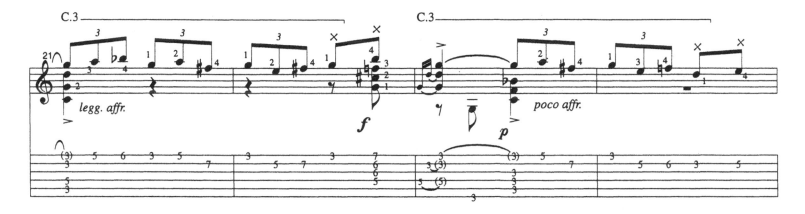

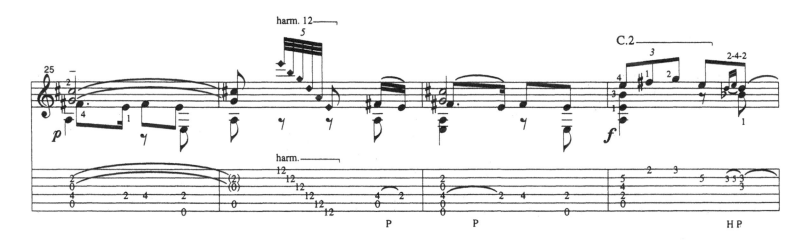

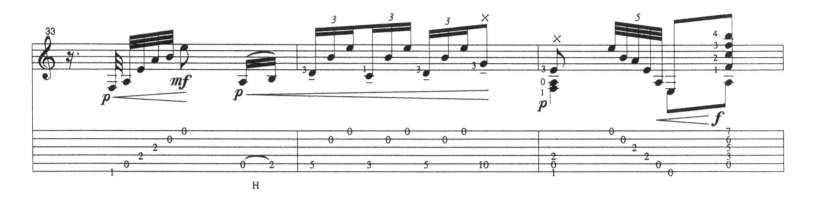

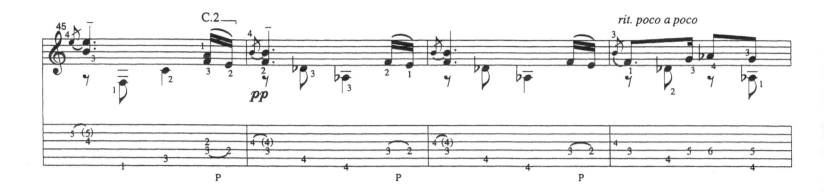

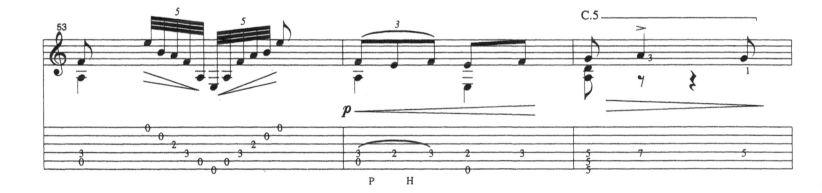

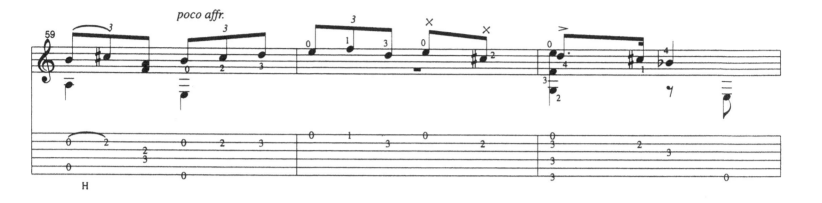

My Lady Hundson's Puffe

John Dowland
(1563–1626)

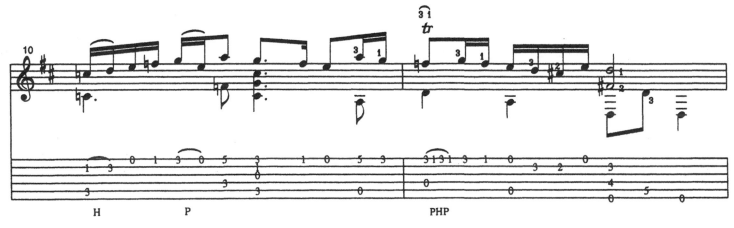

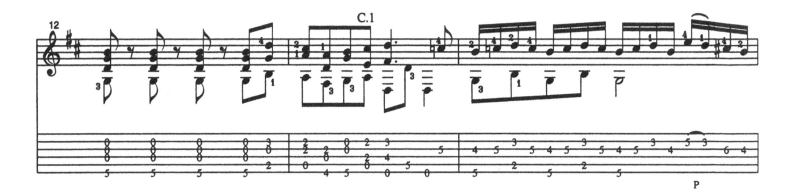

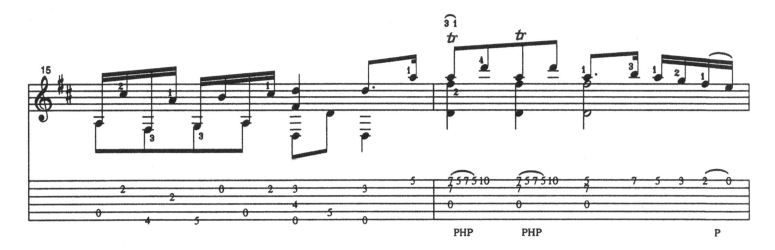

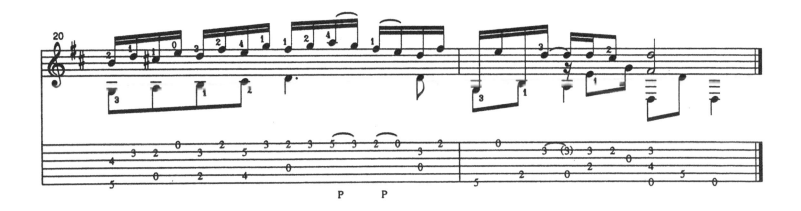

Saltarello in D Major

Vincenzo Galilei
(1520–1591)

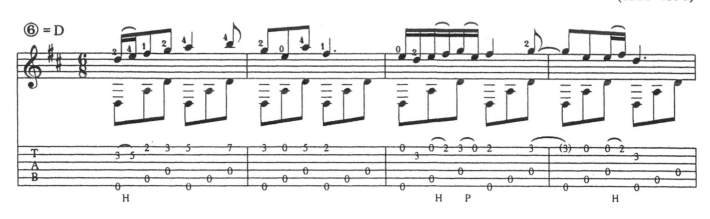

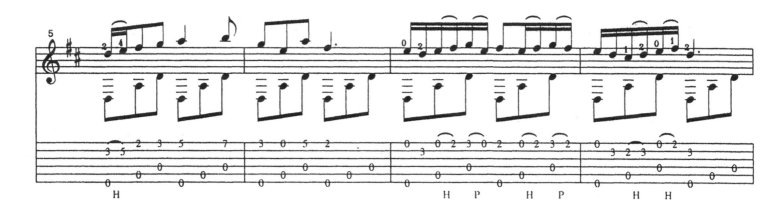

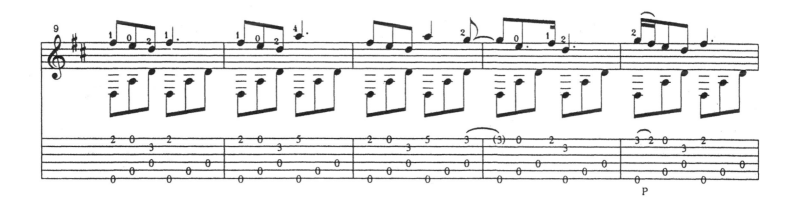

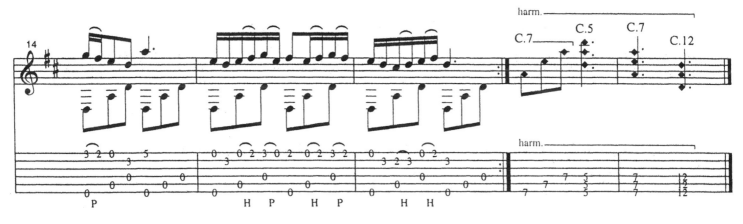

Danza Española No. 10
("Melancolia")

Enrique Granados
(1867-1916)

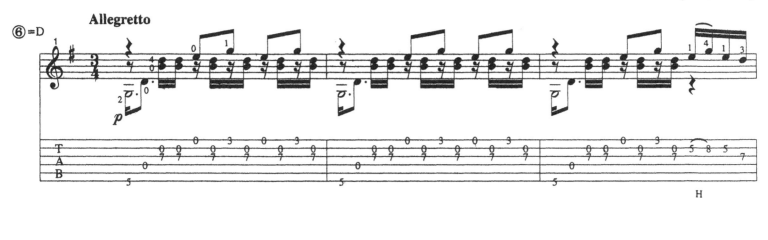

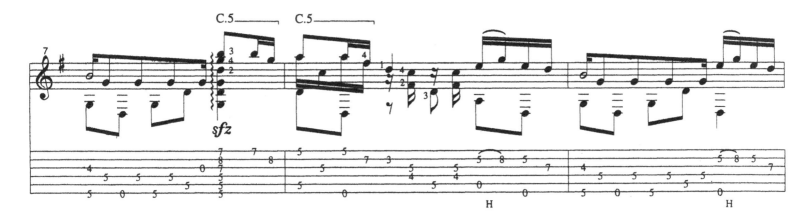

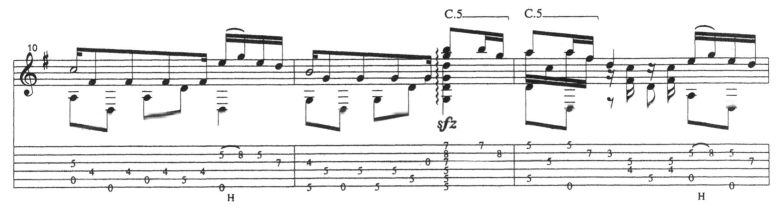

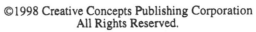

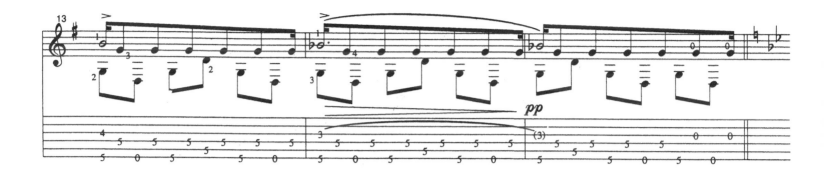

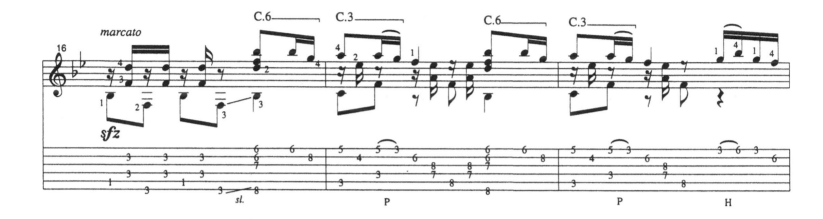

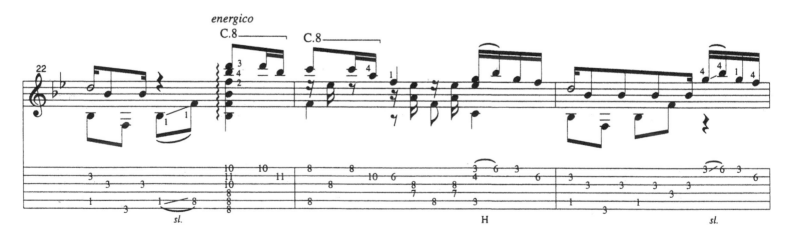

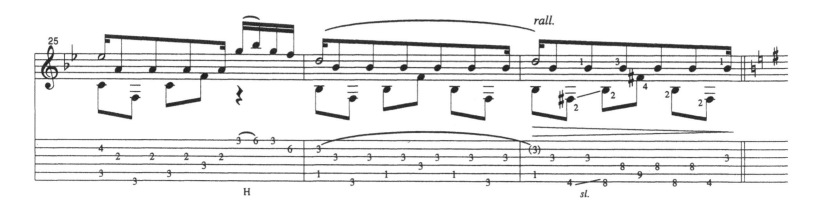

Tempo I

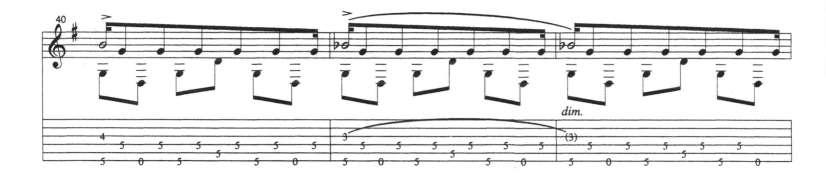

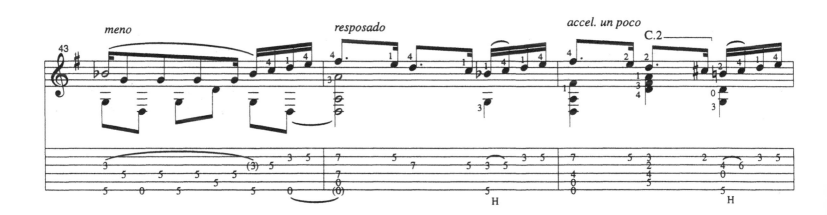

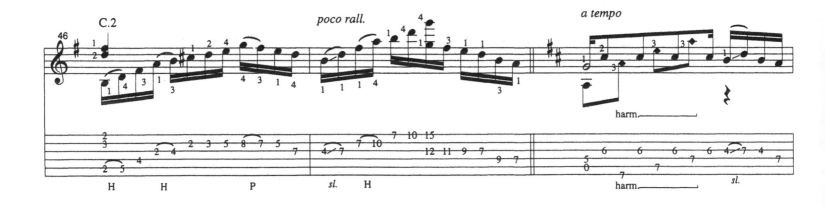

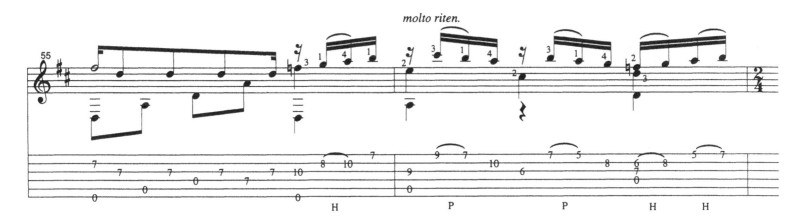

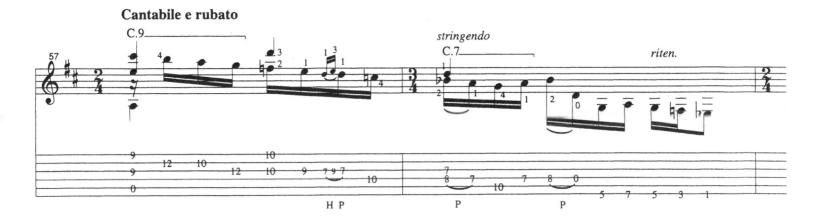

Andante

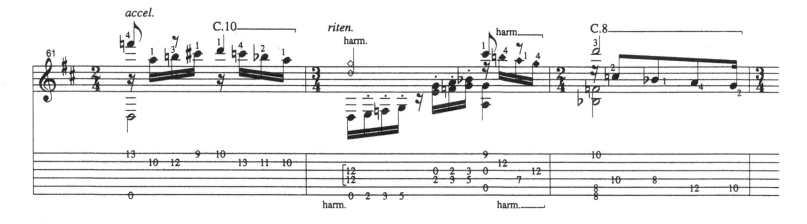

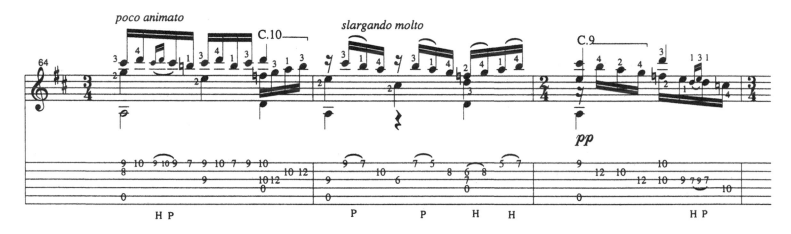

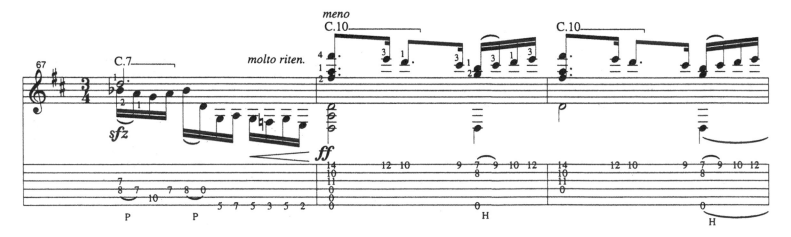

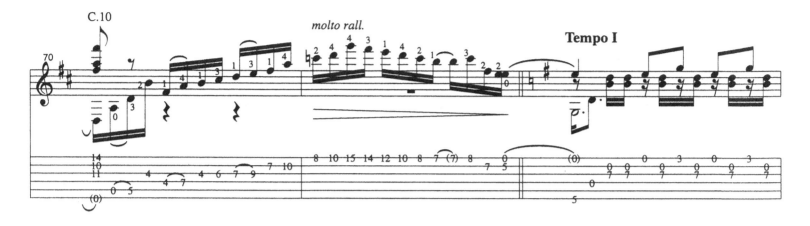

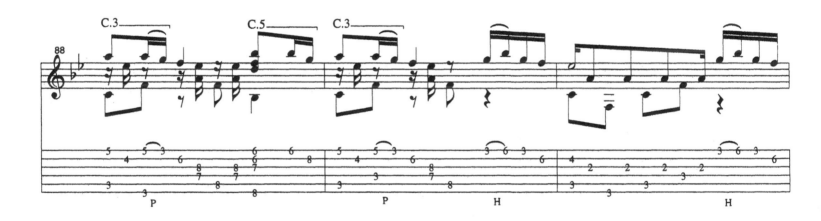

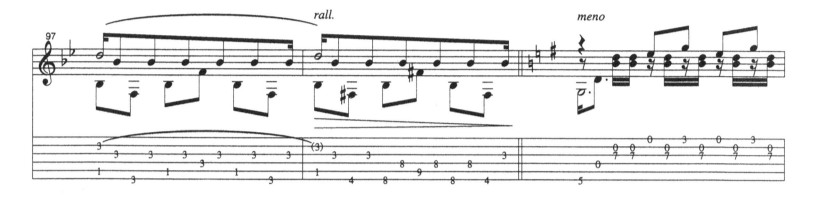

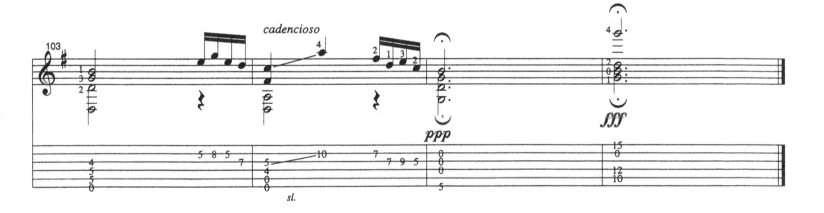

Larghetto
from *Music for the Royal Fireworks*

George Frideric Handel
(1685-1759)

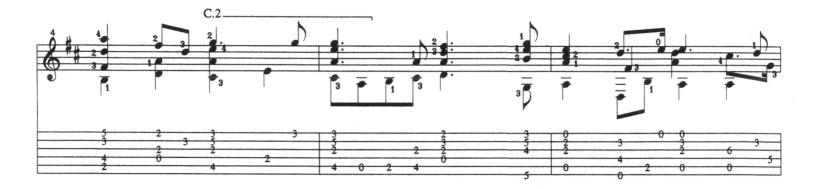

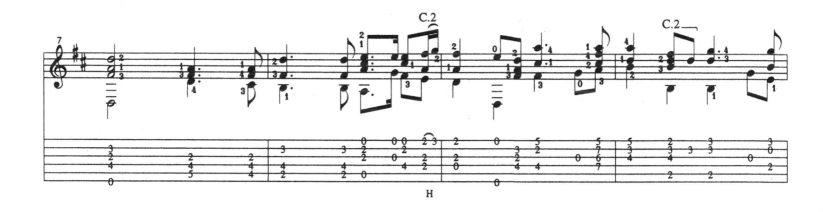

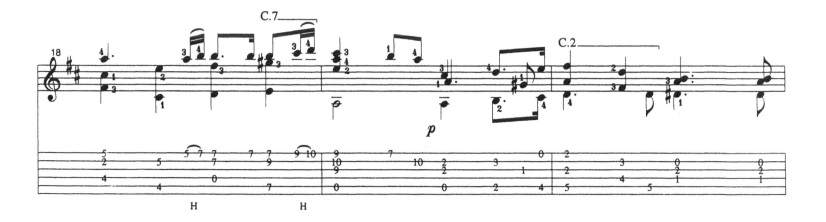

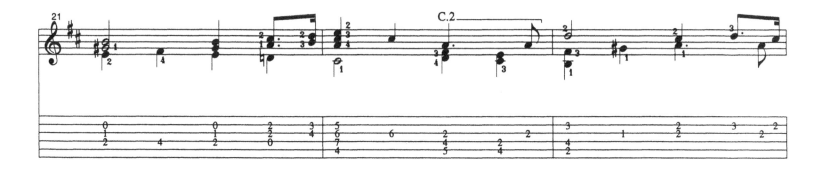

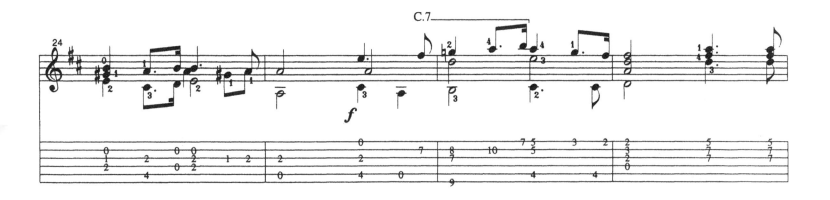

Overture
from *The Messiah*

George Frideric Handel
(1685-1759)

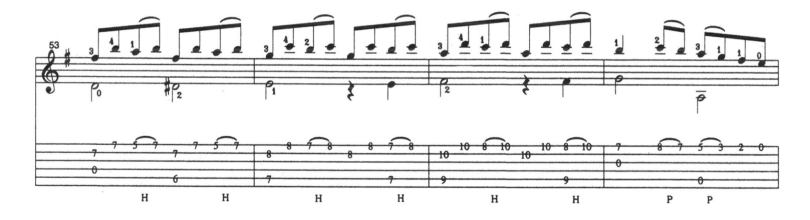

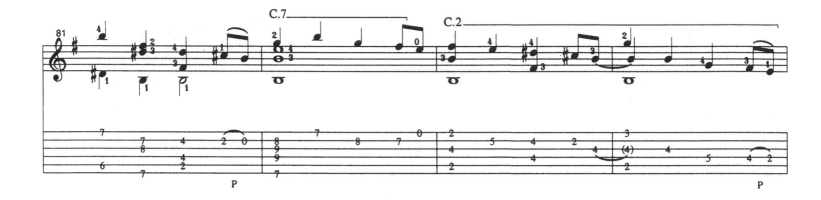

Più lento

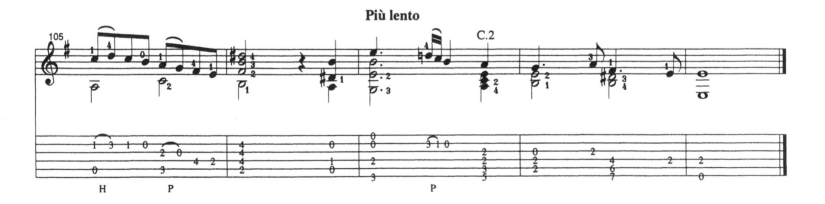

Chaconne

Jan Antonín Losy
(1643/47-1721)

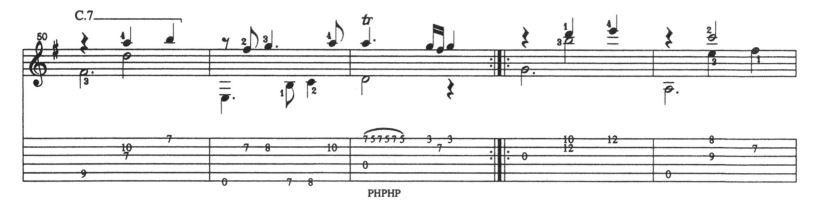

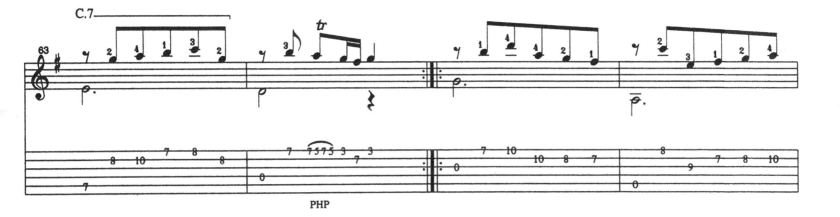

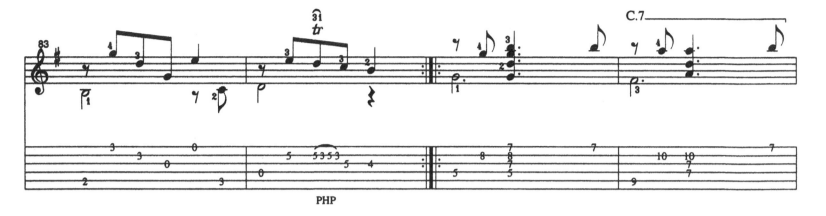

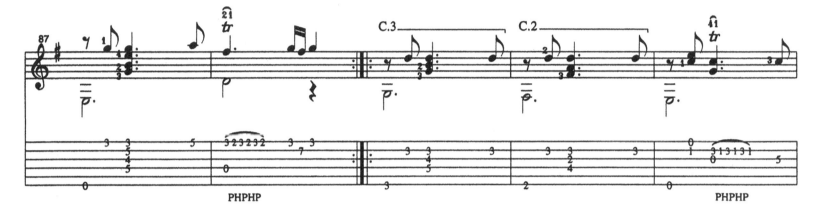

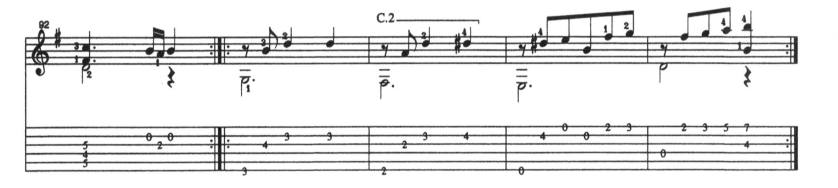

Jig
from *Love and Honour*

Mr. [Thomas] Morgan
(c.1650-c.1710)

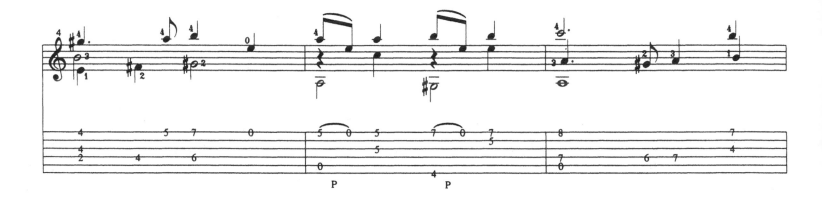

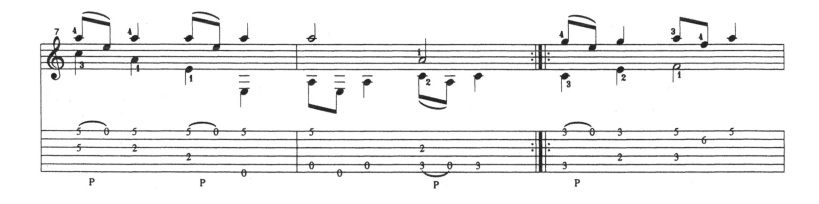

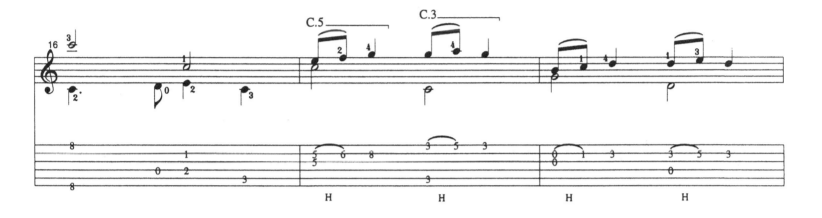

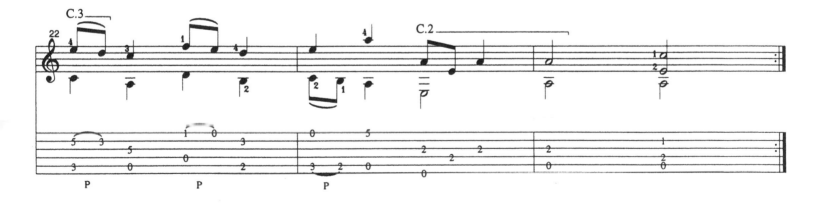

Fantasía No. 10
from *Tres libros de música en cifras para vihuela* (1546)

Alonso de Mudarra
(c.1508–1580)

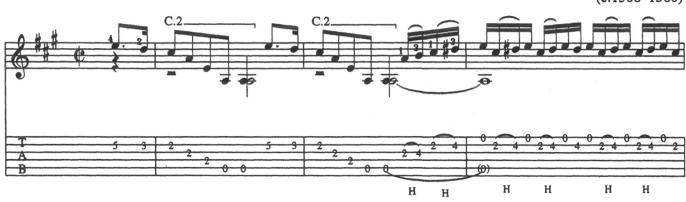

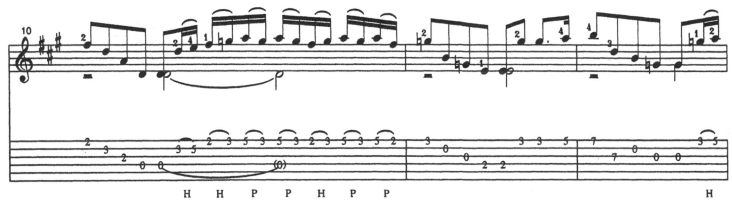

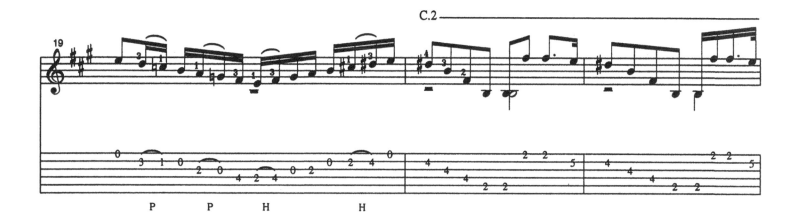

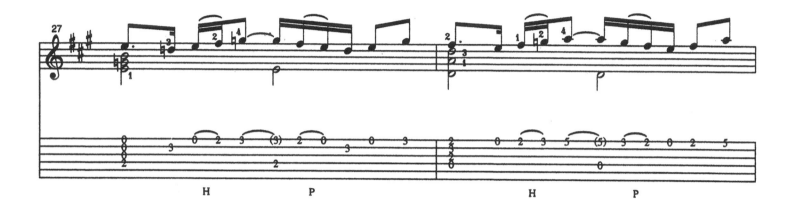

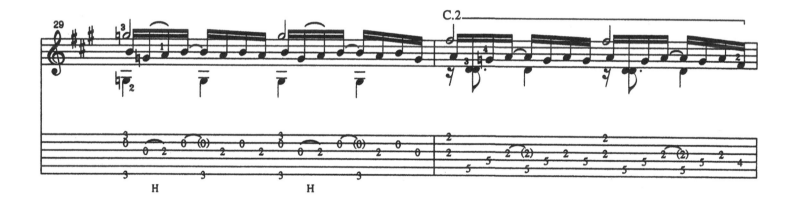

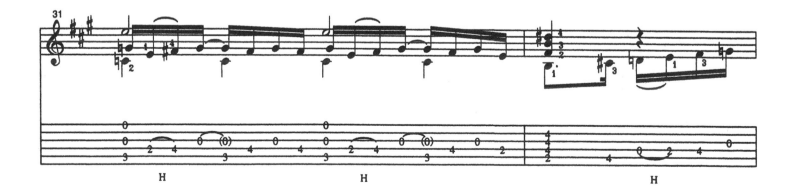

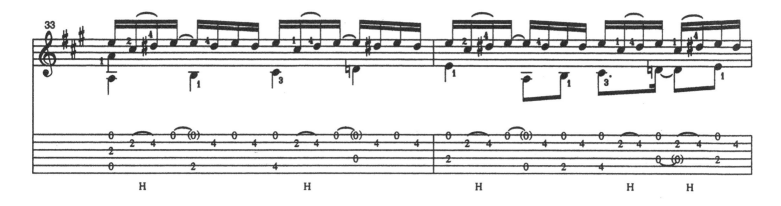

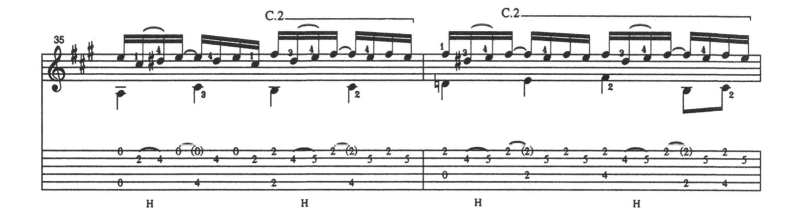

Estrellita
from *Canciones Mexicanos* (1914)

Manuel Ponce
(1882–1948)

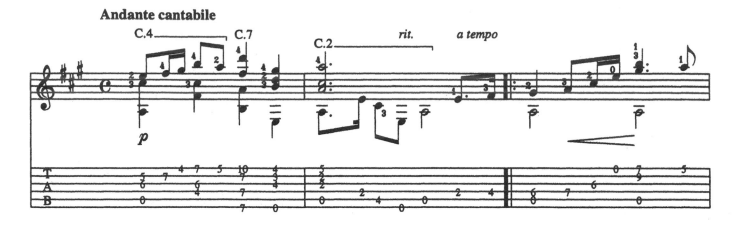

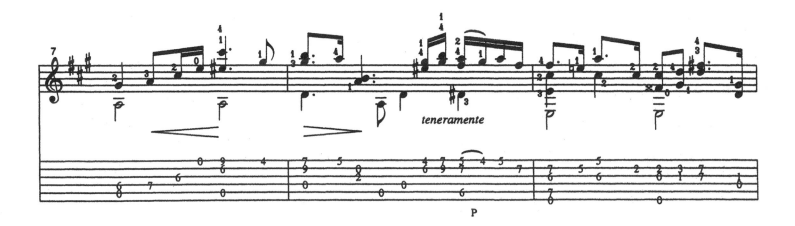

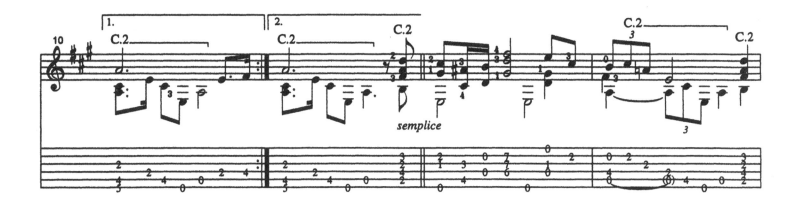

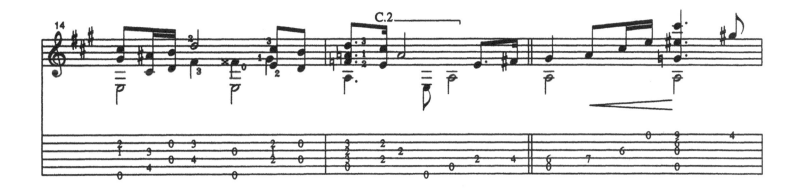

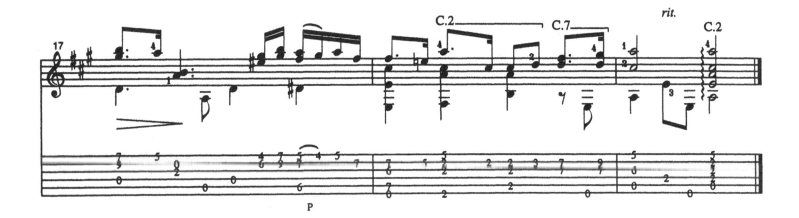

Contredanse en Rondeau
from *Pygmalian*

Jean-Philippe Rameau
(1683-1764)

⑥ = D

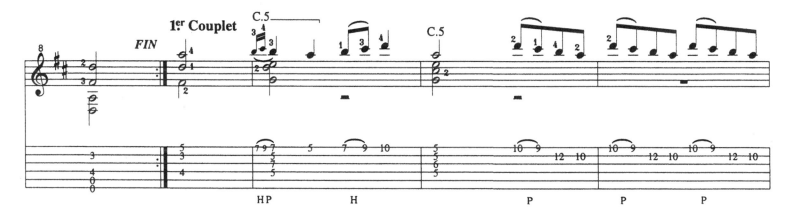

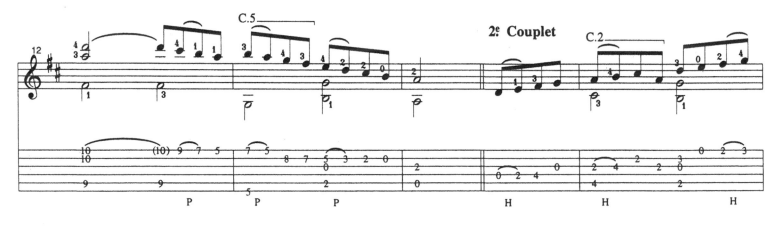

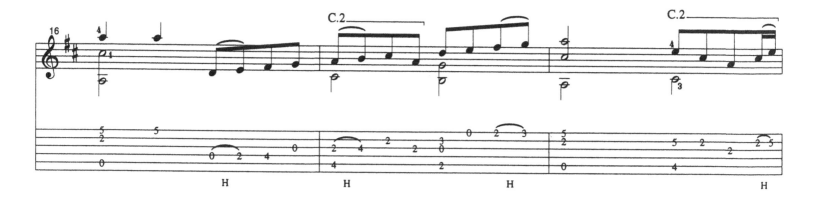

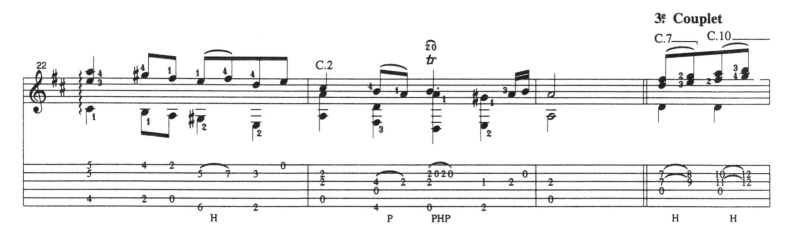

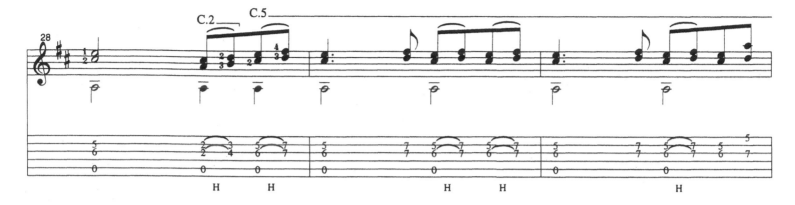

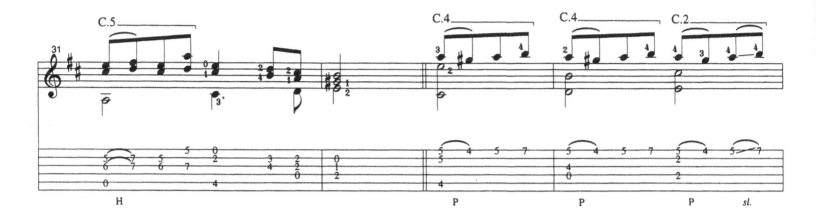

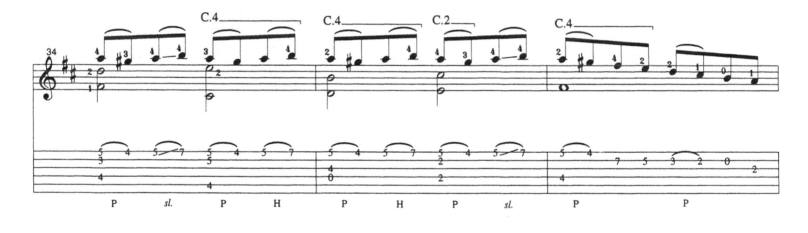

D. S. al Fine

Canarios
from *Instrucción de Música sobre la Guitarra Española* (1674)

Gaspar Sanz
(1640–1710)

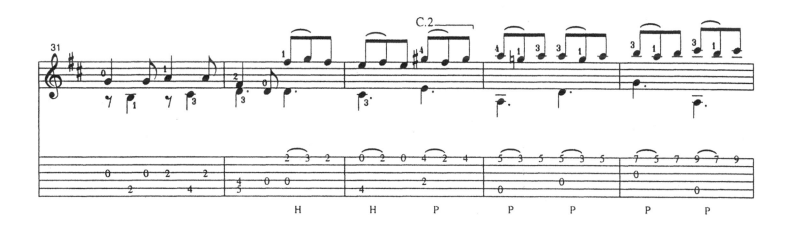

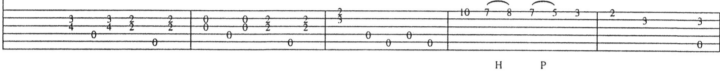
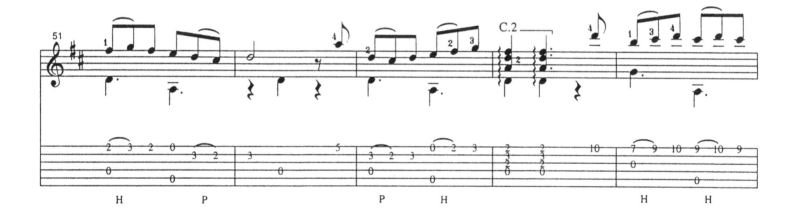
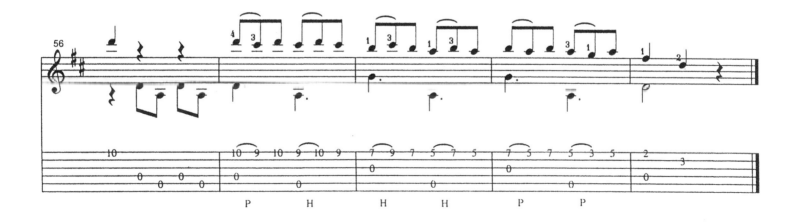

Españoletas

from *Instrucción de Música sobre
la Guitarra Española* (1674)

Gaspar Sanz
(1640–1710)

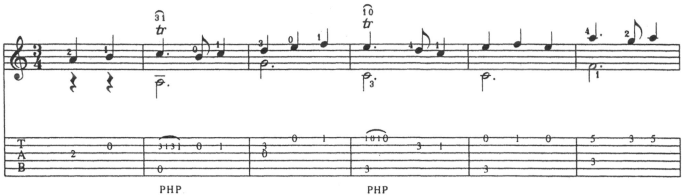

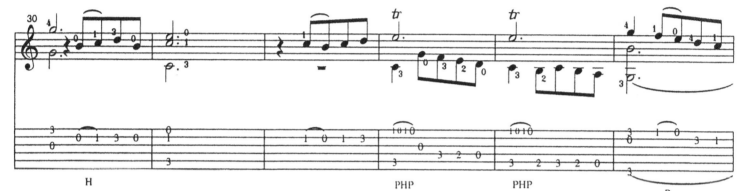

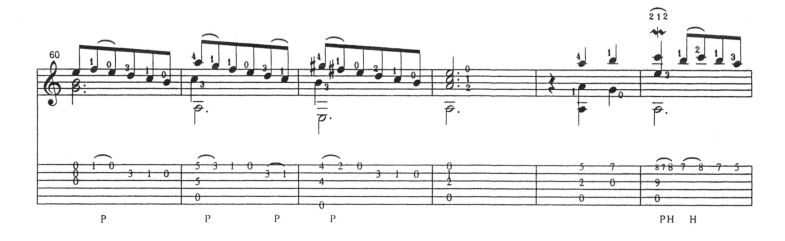

Gymnopédie No. 1
from *Trois Gymnopédies* (1887)

Erik Satie
(1866–1925)

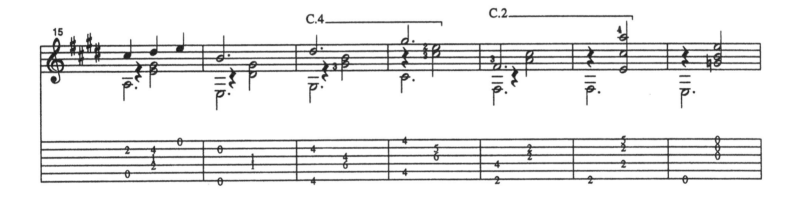

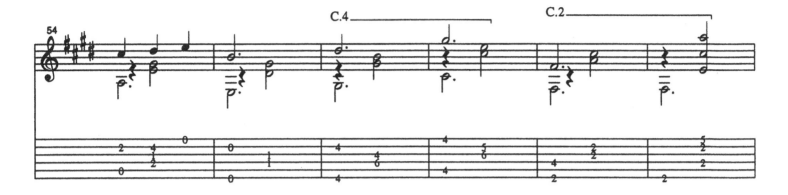

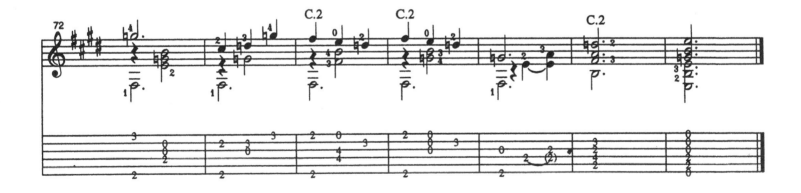

Minuetto
from Toccata No. 4

Alessandro Scarlatti
(1660-1725)

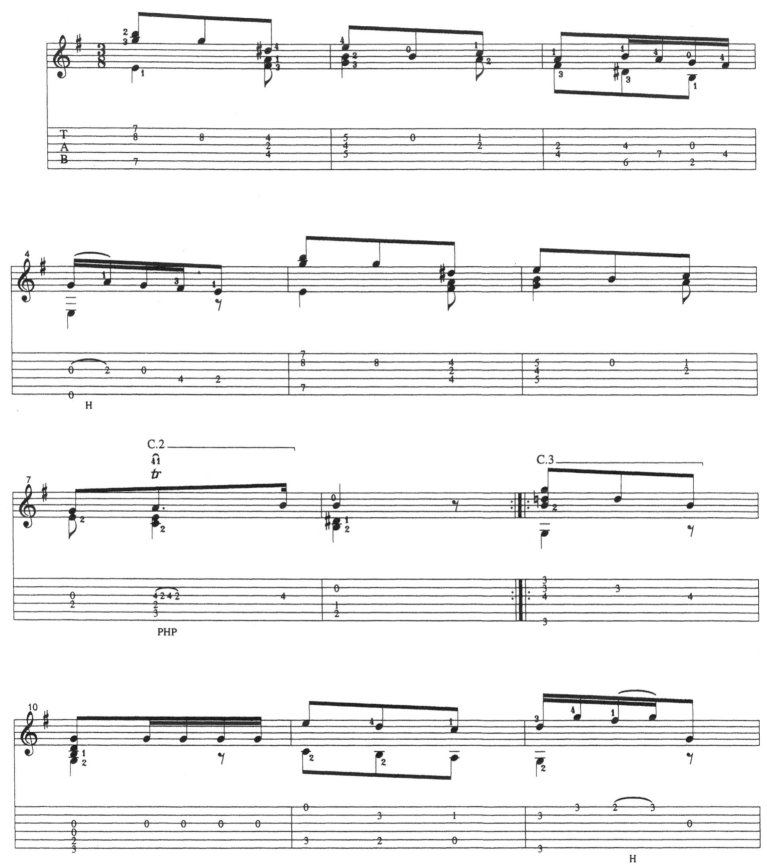

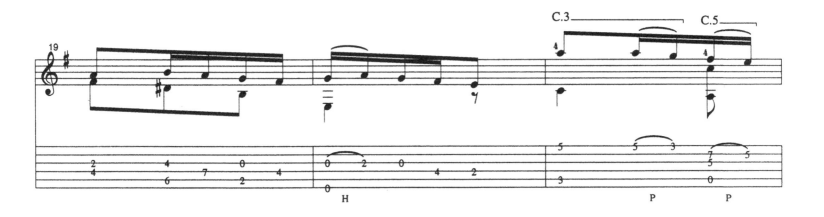

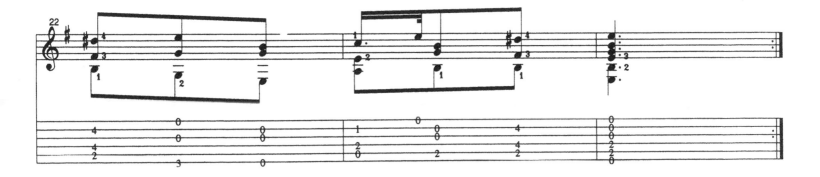

Sonata in A Major
K. 322 (L. 483)

Domenico Scarlatti
(1685–1757)

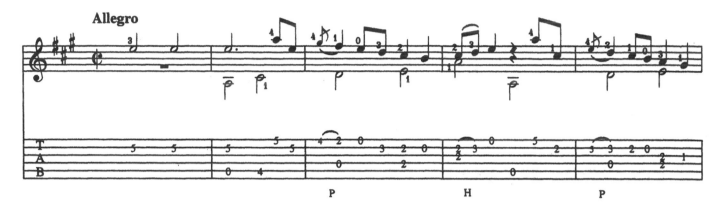

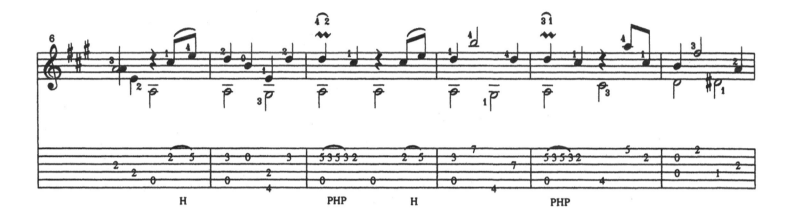

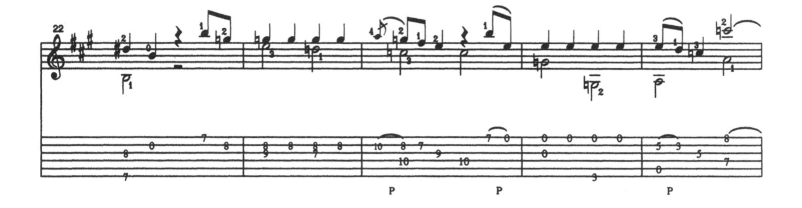

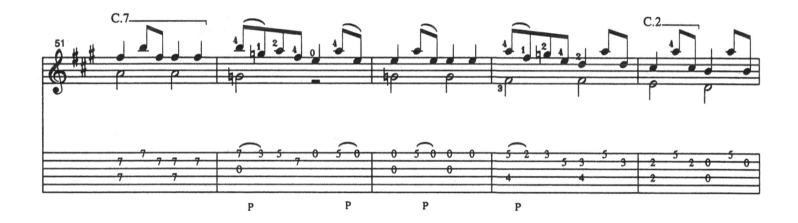

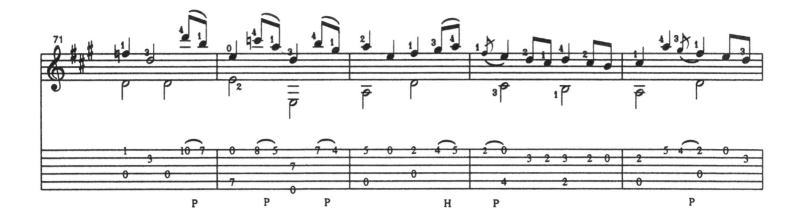

Sonata in G Major
K. 391 (L. 79)

Domenico Scarlatti
(1685–1757)

⑤ = G
⑥ = D

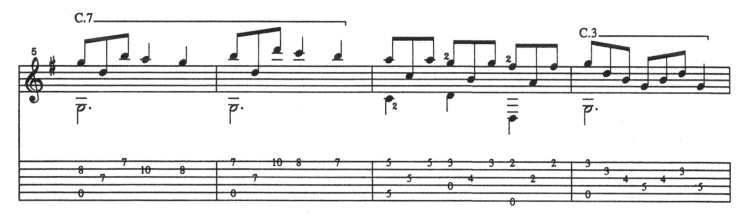

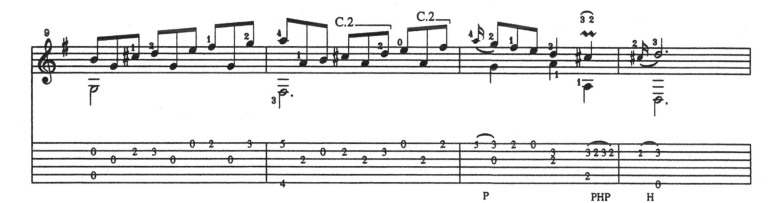

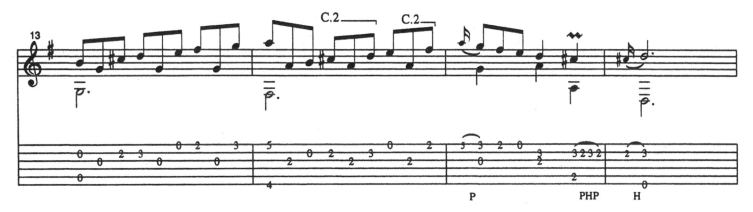

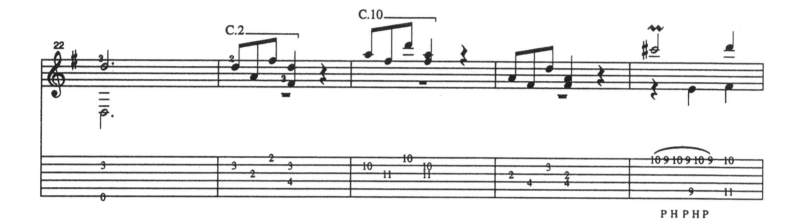

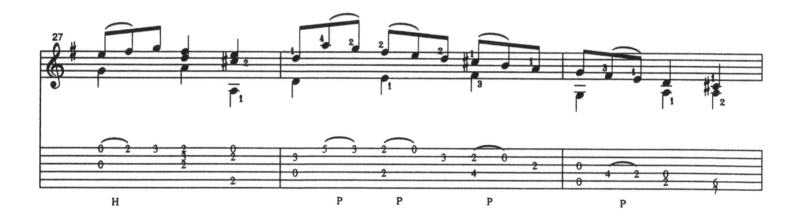

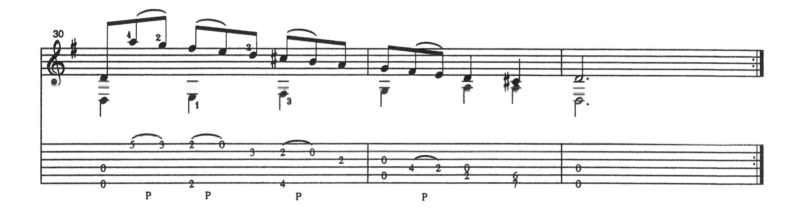

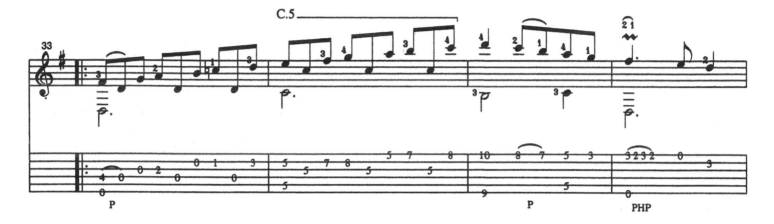

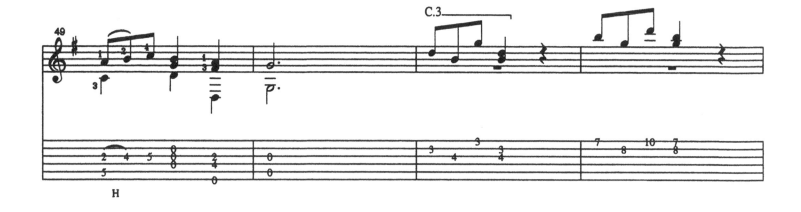

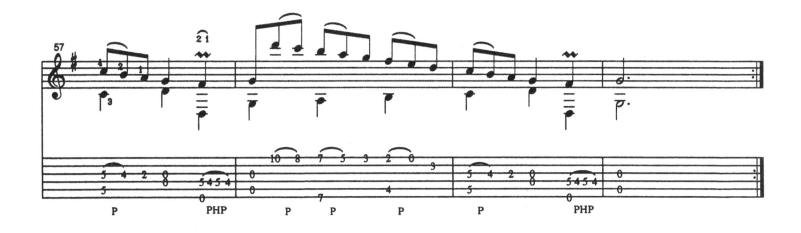

Leçon in D Major
Op. 31, No. 10

Fernando Sor
(1778-1839)

Leçon in E Major
Op. 31, No. 23

Fernando Sor
(1778-1839)

Mouvement de prière religieuse

Minuet in A Major
Opus 11, No. 6

Fernando Sor
(1778-1839)

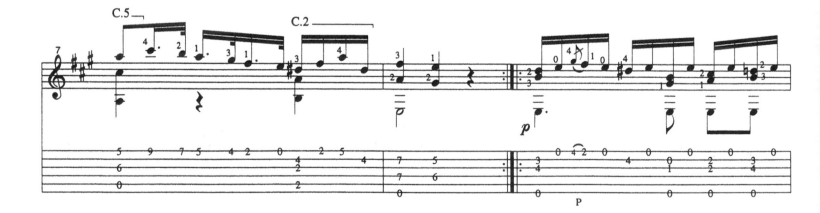

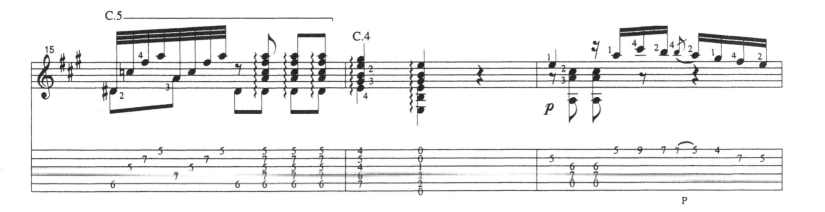

Minuet in G Major
Op. 2, No. 1

Fernando Sor
(1788–1839)

Petite Pièce in E Major
Op. 32, No. 1

Fernando Sor
(1778-1839)

Andantino

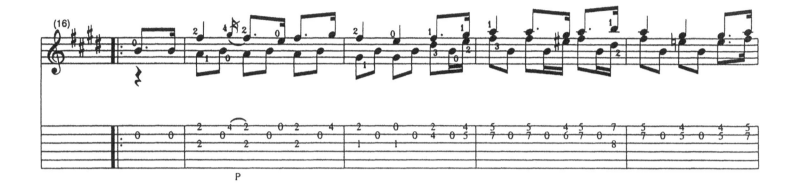

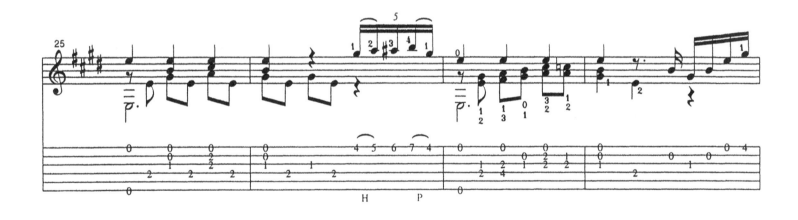

Study in B Minor
Op. 35, No. 22

Fernando Sor
(1788–1839)

Danza Mora

Francisco Tárrega
(1852-1909)

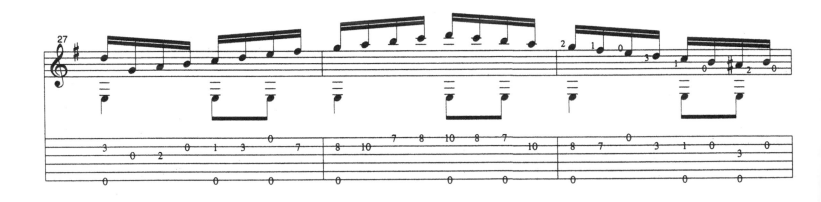

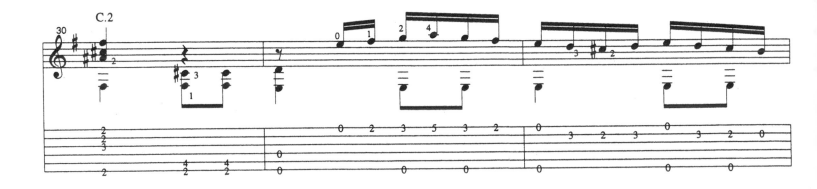

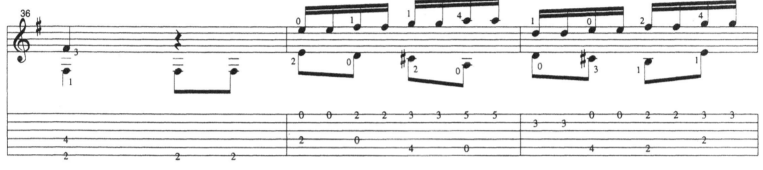

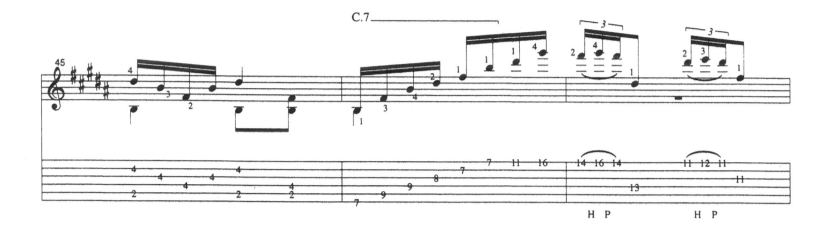

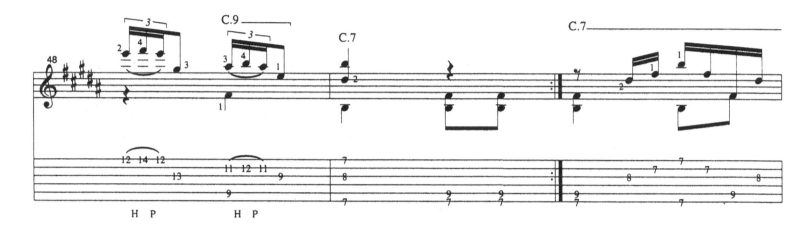

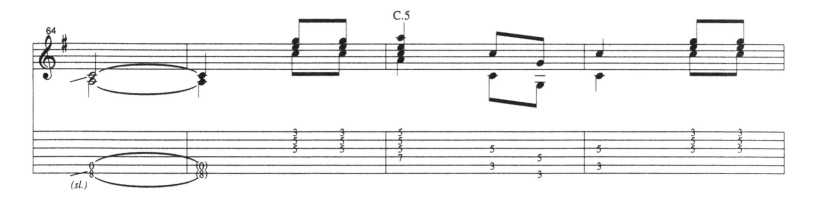

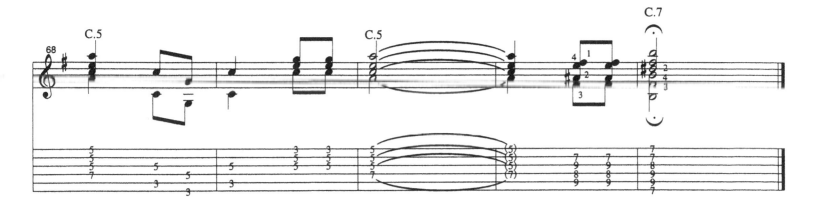

Capricho Arabe
(Serenata)

Francisco Tárrega
(1852-1909)

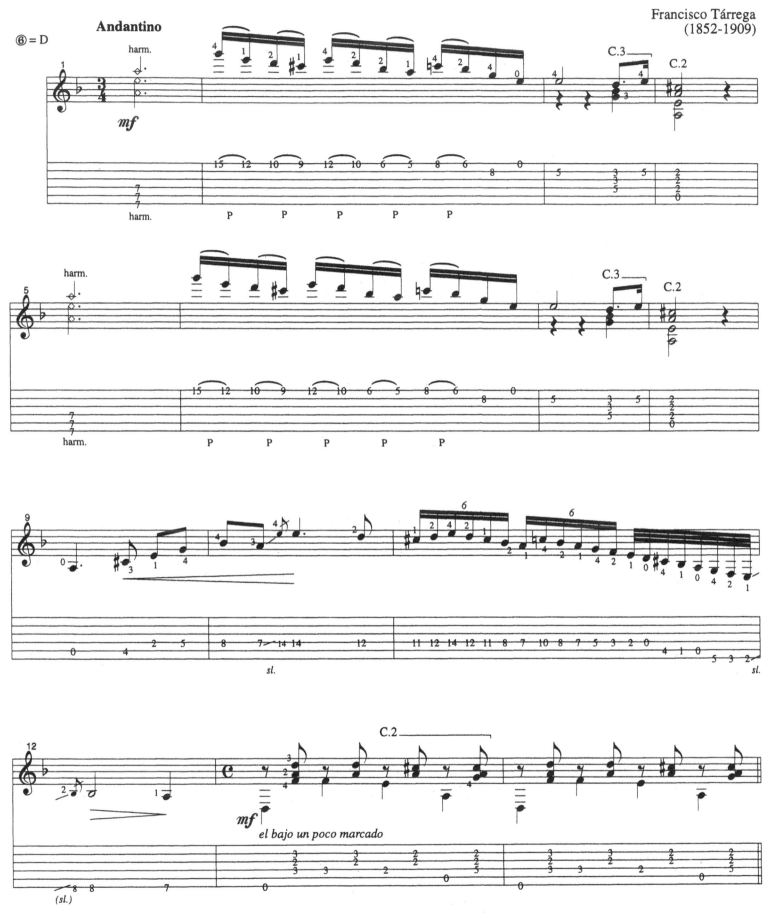

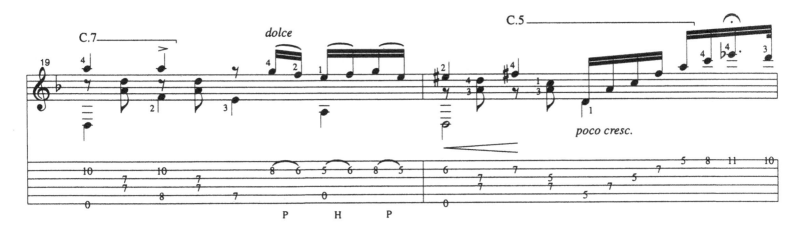

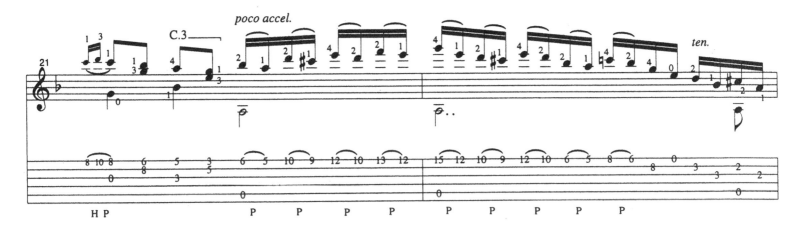

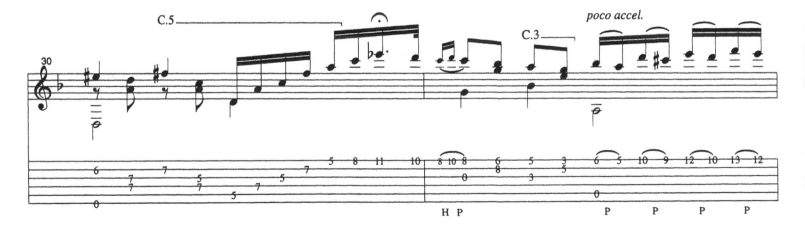

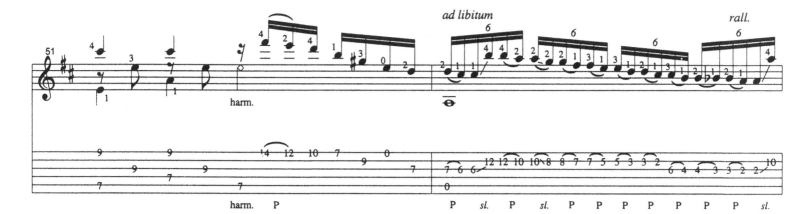

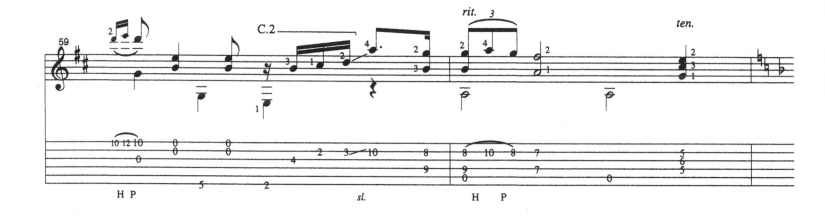

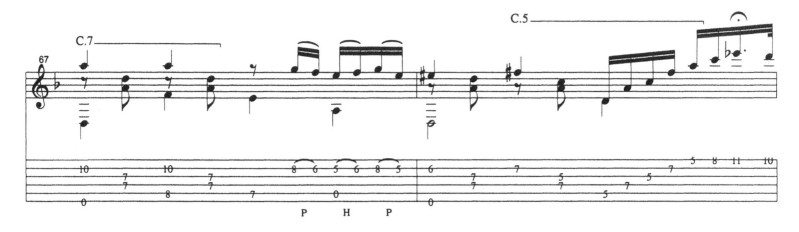

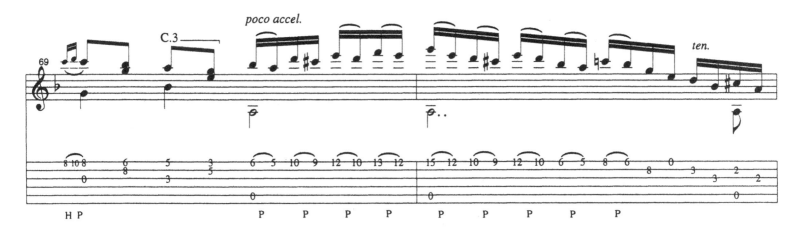

Lágrima
(Preludio)

Francisco Tárrega
(1852–1909)

María
(Gavota)

Francisco Tárrega
(1852-1909)

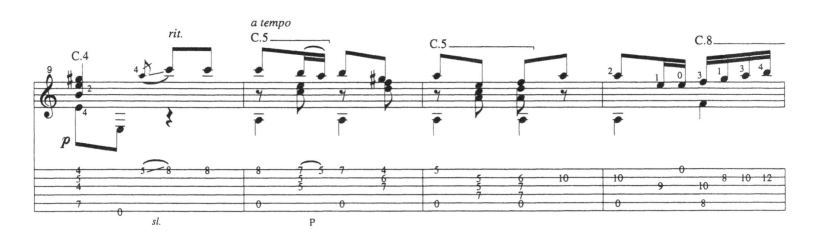

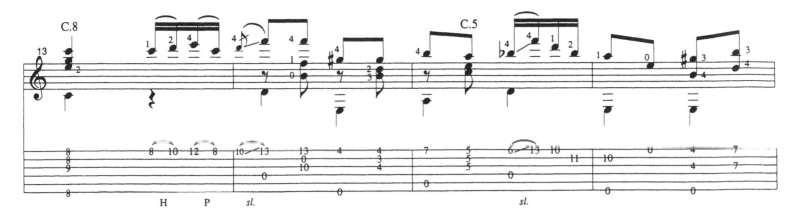

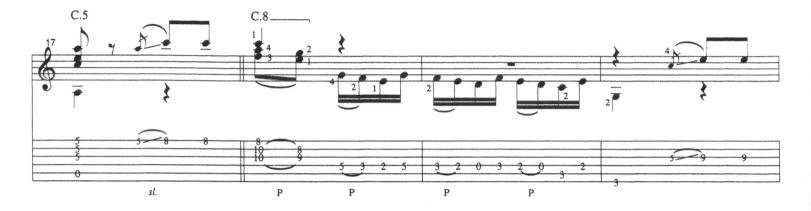

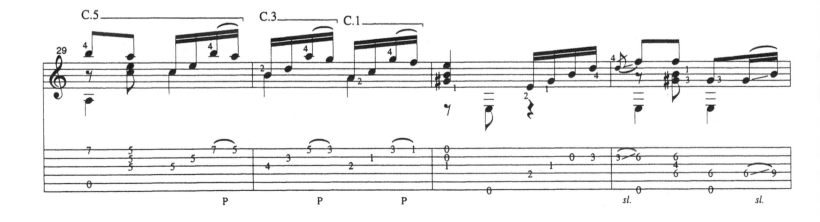

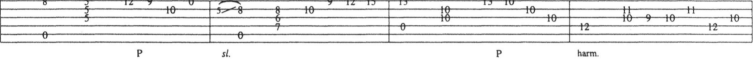

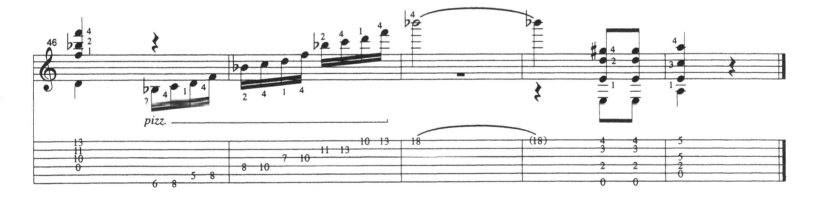

Study in C Major

Francisco Tárrega
(1852–1909)

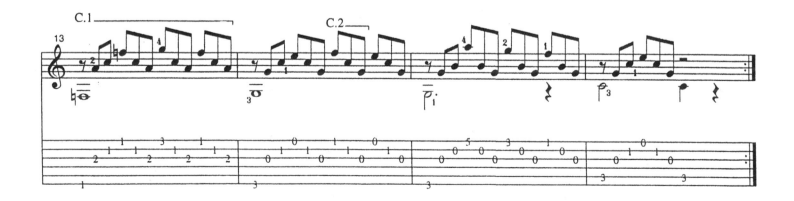

Preludio
from *Sonate d'intavolatura de leuto,* Opus 1

Giovanni Zamboni
(late 1600s-early 1700s)

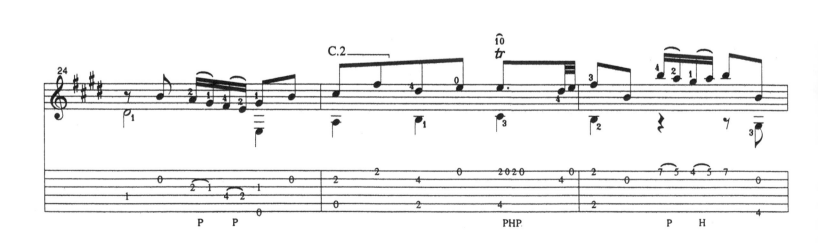

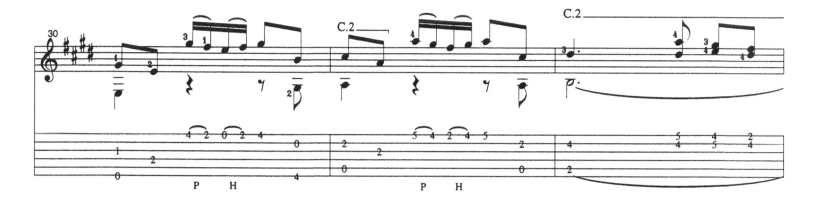

Soneto No. 9
from *Silva de Sirenas* (1547)

Enríquez de Valderrábano
(1500–1557)

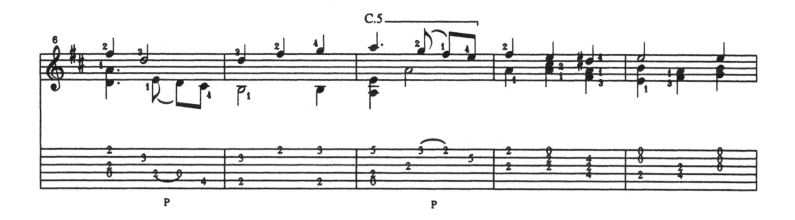

Allegro alla Francese
from Concerto for Violin and Oboe, RV 543

Antonio Vivaldi
(1678-1741)

Allegro non molto
from *The Four Seasons,* Op. 8, No. 2 ("Summer")

Antonio Vivaldi
(1678-1741)

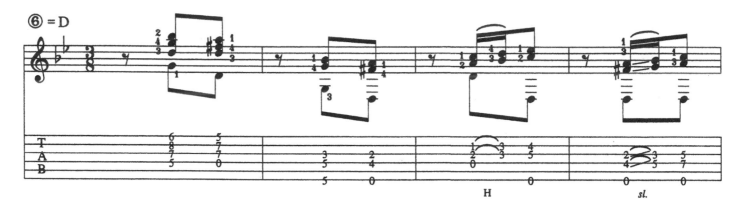

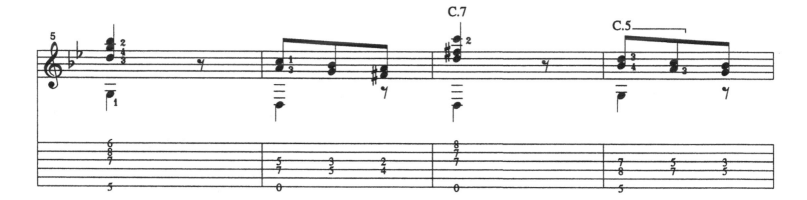

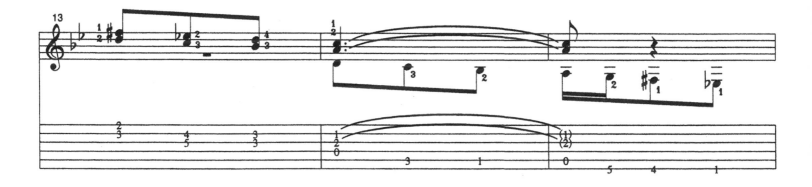

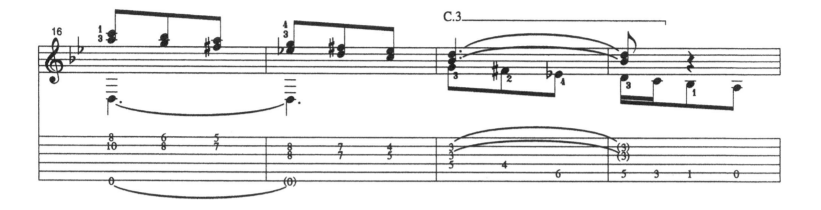

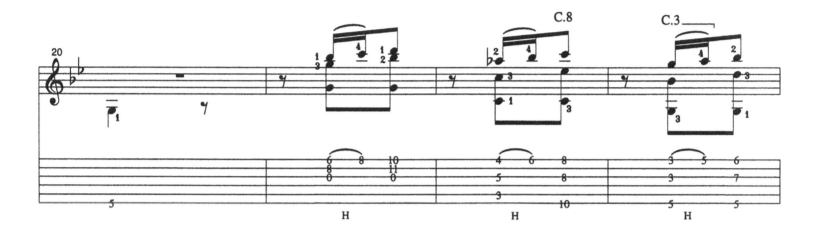

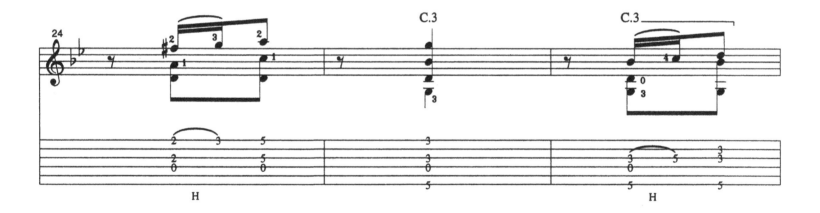

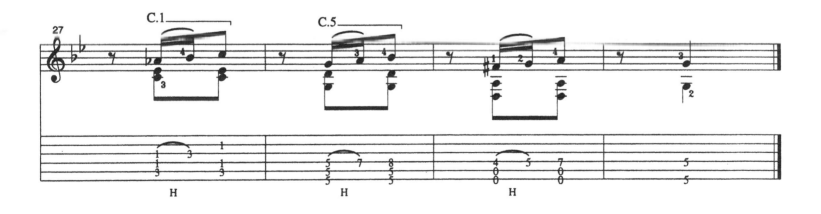

Largo
from *The Four Seasons*, Opus 8, No. 4 ("Winter")

Antonio Vivaldi
(1685-1741)

Bourrée Anglais

Silvius Leopold Weiss
(1686-1750)

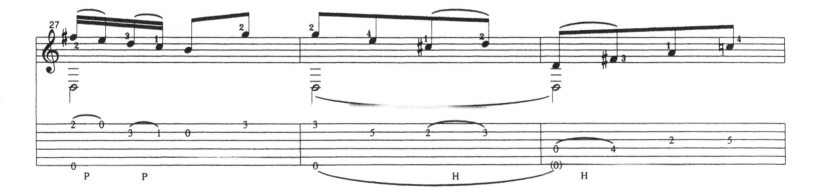

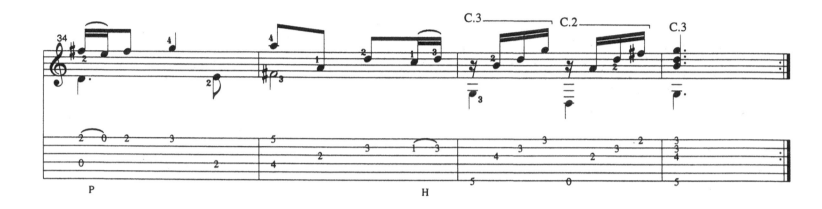

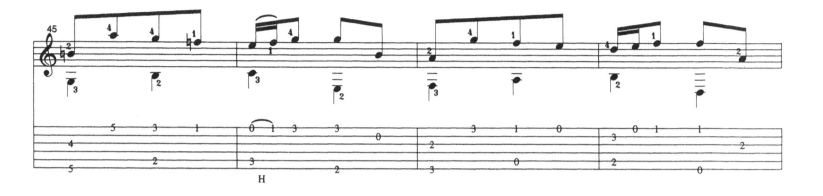

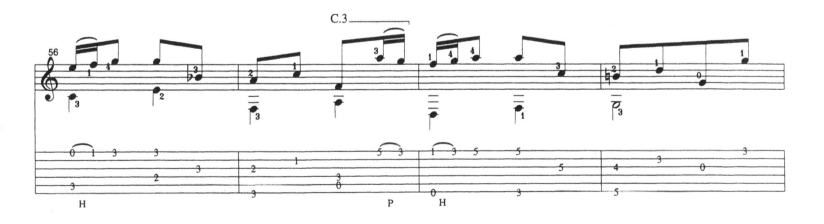

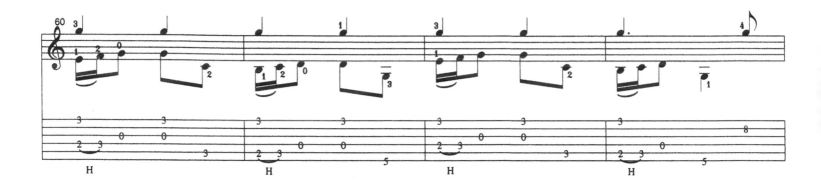

Fantasie

Silvius Leopold Weiss
(1686-1750)

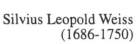

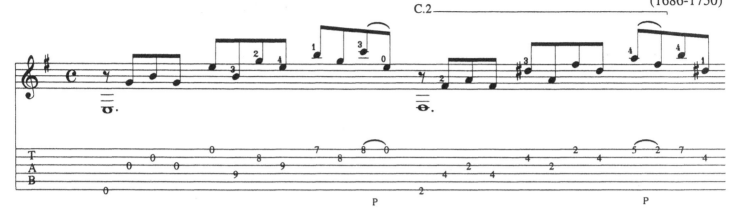

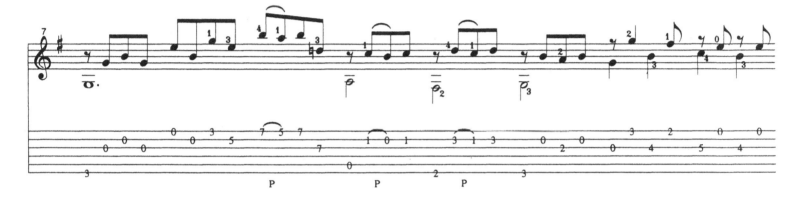

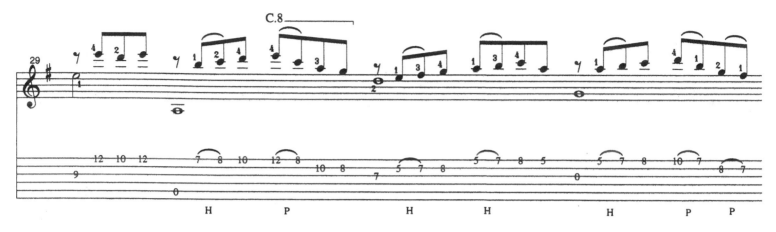

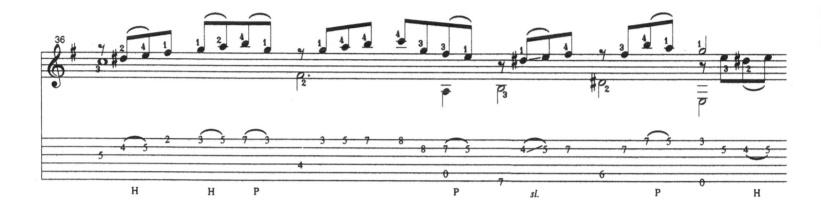

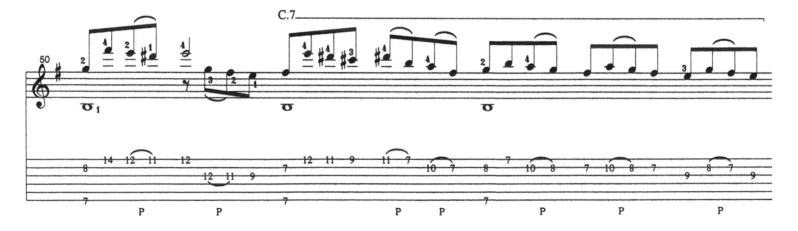

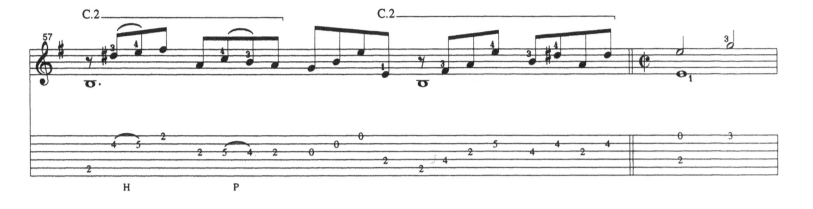

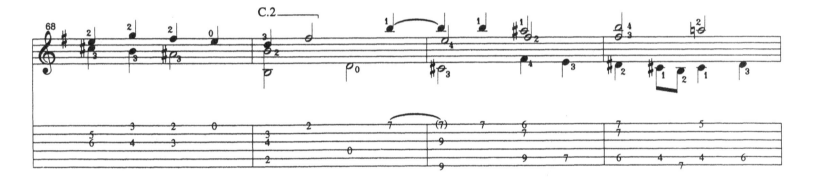

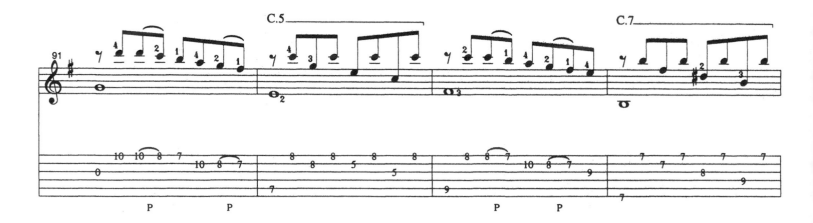

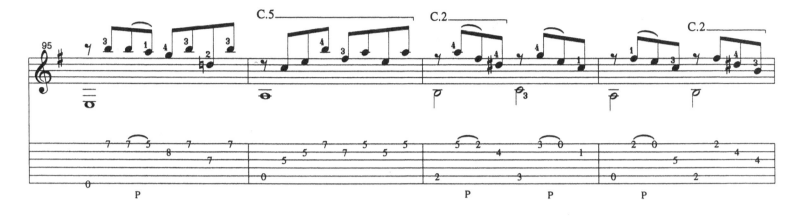

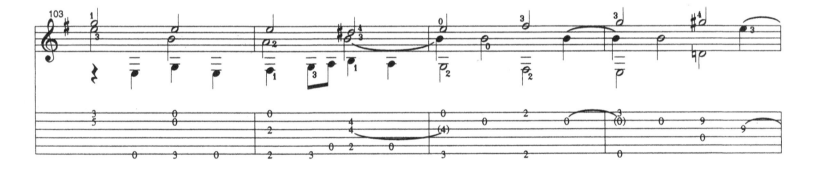

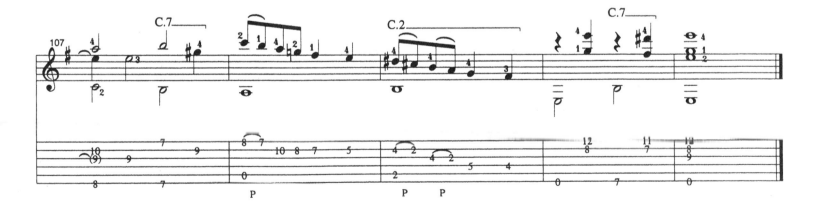

CLASSICAL GUITAR

INSTRUCTIONAL BOOKS & METHODS AVAILABLE FROM HAL LEONARD

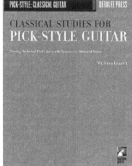

CLASSICAL STUDIES FOR PICK-STYLE GUITAR
by William Leavitt
Berklee Press
This Berklee Workshop, featuring over 20 solos and duets by Bach, Carcassi, Paganini, Sor and other renowned composers, is designed to acquaint intermediate to advanced pick-style guitarists with some of the excellent classical music that is adaptable to pick-style guitar. With study and practice, this workshop will increase a player's knowledge and proficiency on this formidable instrument.
50449440...$12.99

ÉTUDES SIMPLES FOR GUITAR
by Leo Brouwer
Editions Max Eschig
This new, completely revised and updated edition includes critical commentary and performance notes. Each study is accompanied by an introduction that illustrates its principal musical features and technical objectives, complete with suggestions and preparatory exercises.
50565810 Book/CD Pack.......................................$26.99

FIRST BOOK FOR THE GUITAR
by Frederick Noad
G. Schirmer, Inc.
A beginner's manual to the classical guitar. Uses a systematic approach using the interesting solo and duet music written by Noad, one of the world's foremost guitar educators. No musical knowledge is necessary. Student can progress by simple stages. Many of the exercises are designed for a teacher to play with the students. Will increase student's enthusiasm, therefore increasing the desire to take lessons.
50334370 Part 1..$12.99
50334520 Part 2..$17.99
50335160 Part 3..$16.99
50336760 Complete Edition...................................$32.99

HAL LEONARD CLASSICAL GUITAR METHOD
INCLUDES TAB
by Paul Henry
This comprehensive and easy-to-use beginner's guide uses the music of the master composers to teach you the basics of the classical style and technique. Includes pieces by Beethoven, Bach, Mozart, Schumann, Giuliani, Carcassi, Bathioli, Aguado, Tarrega, Purcell, and more. Includes all the basics plus info on PIMA technique, two- and three-part music, time signatures, key signatures, articulation, free stroke, rest stroke, composers, and much more.
00697376 Book/Online Audio (no tab).................$16.99
00142652 Book/Online Audio (with tab)..............$17.99

A MODERN APPROACH TO CLASSICAL GUITAR
by Charles Duncan
This multi-volume method was developed to allow students to study the art of classical guitar within a new, more contemporary framework. For private, class or self-instruction.

00695114 Book 1 – Book Only................................$8.99
00695113 Book 1 – Book/Online Audio...............$12.99
00699204 Book 1 – Repertoire Book Only............$11.99
00699205 Book 1 – Repertoire Book/Online Audio.$16.99
00695116 Book 2 – Book Only................................$7.99
00695115 Book 2 – Book/Online Audio...............$12.99
00699208 Book 2 – Repertoire.............................$12.99
00699202 Book 3 – Book Only................................$9.99
00695117 Book 3 – Book/Online Audio...............$14.99
00695119 Composite Book/CD Pack....................$32.99

100 GRADED CLASSICAL GUITAR STUDIES
Selected and Graded by Frederick Noad
Frederick Noad has selected 100 studies from the works of three outstanding composers of the classical period: Sor, Giuliani, and Carcassi. All these studies are invaluable for developing both right hand and left hand skills. Students and teachers will find this book invaluable for making technical progress. In addition, they will build a repertoire of some of the most melodious music ever written for the guitar.
14023154..$29.99

THE CHRISTOPHER PARKENING GUITAR METHOD, VOL. 1
THE ART AND TECHNIQUE OF THE CLASSICAL GUITAR

CHRISTOPHER PARKENING GUITAR METHOD
THE ART & TECHNIQUE OF THE CLASSICAL GUITAR
Guitarists will learn basic classical technique by playing over 50 beautiful classical pieces, 26 exercises and 14 duets, and through numerous photos and illustrations. The method covers: rudiments of classical technique, note reading and music theory, selection and care of guitars, strategies for effective practicing, and much more!
00696023 Book 1/Online Audio $22.99
00695228 Book 1 (No Audio) $14.99
00696024 Book 2/Online Audio $22.99
00695229 Book 2 (No Audio) $14.99

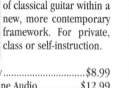

SOLO GUITAR PLAYING
by Frederick M. Noad
Solo Guitar Playing can teach even the person with no previous musical training how to progress from simple single-line melodies to mastery of the guitar as a solo instrument. Fully illustrated with diagrams, photographs, and over 200 musical exercises and repertoire selections, these books offer instruction in every phase of classical guitar playing.
14023147 Book 1/Online Audio $34.99
14023153 Book 1 (Book Only) $24.99
14023151 Book 2 (Book Only) $19.99

TWENTY STUDIES FOR THE GUITAR
ANDRÉS SEGOVIA EDITION
by Fernando Sor
Performed by Paul Henry
20 studies for the classical guitar written by Beethoven's contemporary, Fernando Sor, revised, edited and fingered by the great classical guitarist Andres Segovia. These essential repertoire pieces continue to be used by teachers and students to build solid classical technique. Features 50-minute demonstration audio.
00695012 Book/Online Audio $22.99
00006363 Book Only...$9.99

HAL•LEONARD®
Order these and more publications from your favorite music retailer at
halleonard.com

Prices, contents and availability subject to change without notice.

THE PUBLICATIONS OF
CHRISTOPHER PARKENING

CHRISTOPHER PARKENING – DUETS AND CONCERTOS

Throughout his career, Christopher Parkening has had the opportunity to perform with many of the world's leading artists and orchestras, and this folio contains many selections from those collaborations. All of the pieces included here have been edited and fingered for the guitar by Christopher Parkening himself.

00690938...$24.99

THE CHRISTOPHER PARKENING GUITAR METHOD, VOL. 1 – REVISED

in collaboration with
Jack Marshall and David Brandon

Learn the art of the classical guitar with this premier method for beginners by one of the world's preeminent virtuosos and the recognized heir to the legacy of Andrés Segovia. Learn basic classical guitar technique by playing beautiful pieces of music, including over 50 classical pieces, 26 exercises, and 14 duets. Includes notes in the first position, how to hold the guitar, tuning, right and left hand technique, arpeggios, tone production, placement of fingers and nails, flats, naturals, key signatures, the bar, and more. Also includes many helpful photos and illustrations, plus sections on the history of the classical guitar, selecting a guitar, guitar care, and more.

00695228 Book...$14.99
00696023 Book/Online Audio $22.99

THE CHRISTOPHER PARKENING GUITAR METHOD, VOL. 2

Intermediate to Upper-Intermediate Level

Continues where Vol. 1 leaves off. Teaches: all notes in the upper position; tone production; advanced techniques such as tremolo, harmonics, vibrato, pizzicato and slurs; practice tips; stylistic interpretation; and more. The first half of the book deals primarily with technique, while the second half of the book applies the technique with repertoire pieces. As a special bonus, this book includes 32 previously unpublished Parkening edition pieces by composers including Dowland, Bach, Scarlatti, Sor, Tarrega and other, plus three duets for two guitars.

00695229 Book...$14.99
00696024 Book/Online Audio $22.99

PARKENING AND THE GUITAR – VOL. 1

Music of Two Centuries:
Popular New Transcriptions for Guitar
Virtuoso Music for Guitar

Ten transcriptions for solo guitar of beautiful music from many periods and styles, edited and fingered by Christopher Parkening. All pieces are suitable for performance by the advanced guitarist. Ten selections: Afro-Cuban Lullaby • Empress of the Pagodes (Ravel) • Menuet (Ravel) • Minuet in D (Handel) • Passacaille (Weiss) • Pastourelle (Poulenc) • Pavane for a Dead Princess (Ravel) • Pavane for a Sleeping Beauty (Ravel) • Preambulo (Scarlatti-Ponce) • Sarabande (Handel).

00699105...$9.95

PARKENING AND THE GUITAR – VOL. 2

Music of Two Centuries:
Popular New Transcriptions for Guitar
Virtuoso Music for Guitar

Nine more selections for the advanced guitarist: Clair de Lune (Debussy) • Giga (Visée) • The Girl with the Flaxen Hair (Debussy) • Gymnopedie Nos. I-III (Satie) • The Little Shepherd (Debussy) • The Mysterious Barricades (Couperin) • Sarabande (Debussy).

00699106...$9.95

CHRISTOPHER PARKENING – ROMANZA

Virtuoso Music for Guitar

Three wonderful transcriptions edited and fingered by Parkening: Catalonian Song • Rumores de la Caleta • Romance.

00699103...$10.99

CHRISTOPHER PARKENING – SACRED MUSIC FOR THE GUITAR, VOL. 1

Seven inspirational arrangements, transcriptions and compositions covering traditional Christian melodies from several centuries. These selections appear on the Parkening album Sacred Music for the Guitar. Includes: Präludium (Bach) • Our Great Savior • God of Grace and God of Glory (2 guitars) • Brethren, We Have Met to Worship • Deep River • Jesus, We Want to Meet • Evening Prayer.

00699095...$14.99

CHRISTOPHER PARKENING – SACRED MUSIC FOR THE GUITAR, VOL. 2

Seven more selections from the album *Sacred Music for the Guitar:* Hymn of Christian Joy (guitar and harpsichord) • Simple Gifts • Fairest Lord Jesus • Stir Thy Church, O God Our Father • All Creatures of Our God and King • Glorious Things of Thee Are Spoken • Praise Ye the Lord (2 guitars).

00699100...$15.99

CHRISTOPHER PARKENING – SOLO PIECES

Sixteen transcriptions for solo guitar edited and fingered by Parkening, including: Allegro • Danza • Fugue • Galliard • I Stand at the Threshold • Prelude • Sonata in D • Suite Española • Suite in D Minor • and more.

00690939...$24.99

PARKENING PLAYS BACH

Virtuoso Music for Guitar

Nine transcriptions edited and fingered by Parkening: Preludes I, VI & IX • Gavottes I & II • Jesu, Joy of Man's Desiring • Sheep May Safely Graze • Wachet Auf, Ruft Uns Die Stemme • Be Thou with Me • Sleepers Awake (2 guitars).

00699104...$9.95

CHRISTOPHER PARKENING – VIRTUOSO PERFORMANCES

This DVD features performances and career highlights from classical guitar virtuoso Christopher Parkening (filmed in 1971, 1973, 1998 and 2003). Viewers can watch feature titles in their entirety or select individual songs. As a bonus, there is archival footage of Andrés Segovia performing in studio, circa 1950. The DVD also includes an informational booklet. 95 minutes.

00320506 DVD $24.99

HAL•LEONARD®

www.halleonard.com

EASY GUITAR WITH NOTES & TAB

This series features simplified arrangements with notes, tab, chord charts, and strum and pick patterns.

MIXED FOLIOS

00702287	Acoustic	$19.99
00702002	Acoustic Rock Hits for Easy Guitar	$15.99
00702166	All-Time Best Guitar Collection	$19.99
00702232	Best Acoustic Songs for Easy Guitar	$16.99
00119835	Best Children's Songs	$16.99
00703055	The Big Book of Nursery Rhymes & Children's Songs	$16.99
00698978	Big Christmas Collection	$19.99
00702394	Bluegrass Songs for Easy Guitar	$15.99
00289632	Bohemian Rhapsody	$19.99
00703387	Celtic Classics	$16.99
00224808	Chart Hits of 2016-2017	$14.99
00267383	Chart Hits of 2017-2018	$14.99
00334293	Chart Hits of 2019-2020	$16.99
00403479	Chart Hits of 2021-2022	$16.99
00702149	Children's Christian Songbook	$9.99
00702028	Christmas Classics	$8.99
00101779	Christmas Guitar	$14.99
00702141	Classic Rock	$8.95
00159642	Classical Melodies	$12.99
00253933	Disney/Pixar's Coco	$16.99
00702203	CMT's 100 Greatest Country Songs	$34.99
00702283	The Contemporary Christian Collection	$16.99

00196954	Contemporary Disney	$19.99
00702239	Country Classics for Easy Guitar	$24.99
00702257	Easy Acoustic Guitar Songs	$17.99
00702041	Favorite Hymns for Easy Guitar	$12.99
00222701	Folk Pop Songs	$17.99
00126894	Frozen	$14.99
00333922	Frozen 2	$14.99
00702286	Glee	$16.99
00702160	The Great American Country Songbook	$19.99
00702148	Great American Gospel for Guitar	$14.99
00702050	Great Classical Themes for Easy Guitar	$9.99
00275088	The Greatest Showman	$17.99
00148030	Halloween Guitar Songs	$14.99
00702273	Irish Songs	$14.99
00192503	Jazz Classics for Easy Guitar	$16.99
00702275	Jazz Favorites for Easy Guitar	$17.99
00702274	Jazz Standards for Easy Guitar	$19.99
00702162	Jumbo Easy Guitar Songbook	$24.99
00232285	La La Land	$16.99
00702258	Legends of Rock	$14.99
00702189	MTV's 100 Greatest Pop Songs	$34.99
00702272	1950s Rock	$16.99
00702271	1960s Rock	$16.99
00702270	1970s Rock	$24.99
00702269	1980s Rock	$16.99

00702268	1990s Rock	$24.99
00369043	Rock Songs for Kids	$14.99
00109725	Once	$14.99
00702187	Selections from O Brother Where Art Thou?	$19.99
00702178	100 Songs for Kids	$16.99
00702515	Pirates of the Caribbean	$17.99
00702125	Praise and Worship for Guitar	$14.99
00287930	Songs from *A Star Is Born, The Greatest Showman, La La Land*, and More Movie Musicals	$16.99
00702285	Southern Rock Hits	$12.99
00156420	Star Wars Music	$16.99
00121535	30 Easy Celtic Guitar Solos	$16.99
00244654	Top Hits of 2017	$14.99
00283786	Top Hits of 2018	$14.99
00302269	Top Hits of 2019	$14.99
00355779	Top Hits of 2020	$14.99
00374083	Top Hits of 2021	$16.99
00702294	Top Worship Hits	$17.99
00702255	VH1's 100 Greatest Hard Rock Songs	$34.99
00702175	VH1's 100 Greatest Songs of Rock and Roll	$34.99
00702253	Wicked	$12.99

ARTIST COLLECTIONS

00702267	AC/DC for Easy Guitar	$16.99
00156221	Adele – 25	$16.99
00396889	Adele – 30	$19.99
00702040	Best of the Allman Brothers	$16.99
00702865	J.S. Bach for Easy Guitar	$15.99
00702169	Best of The Beach Boys	$16.99
00702292	The Beatles — 1	$22.99
00125796	Best of Chuck Berry	$16.99
00702201	The Essential Black Sabbath	$15.99
00702250	blink-182 — Greatest Hits	$17.99
02501615	Zac Brown Band — The Foundation	$17.99
02501621	Zac Brown Band — You Get What You Give	$16.99
00702043	Best of Johnny Cash	$17.99
00702090	Eric Clapton's Best	$16.99
00702086	Eric Clapton — from the Album Unplugged	$17.99
00702202	The Essential Eric Clapton	$17.99
00702053	Best of Patsy Cline	$17.99
00222697	Very Best of Coldplay – 2nd Edition	$17.99
00702229	The Very Best of Creedence Clearwater Revival	$16.99
00702145	Best of Jim Croce	$16.99
00702278	Crosby, Stills & Nash	$12.99
14042809	Bob Dylan	$15.99
00702276	Fleetwood Mac — Easy Guitar Collection	$17.99
00139462	The Very Best of Grateful Dead	$16.99
00702136	Best of Merle Haggard	$16.99
00702227	Jimi Hendrix — Smash Hits	$19.99
00702288	Best of Hillsong United	$12.99
00702236	Best of Antonio Carlos Jobim	$15.99

00702245	Elton John — Greatest Hits 1970–2002	$19.99
00129855	Jack Johnson	$17.99
00702204	Robert Johnson	$16.99
00702234	Selections from Toby Keith — 35 Biggest Hits	$12.95
00702003	Kiss	$16.99
00702216	Lynyrd Skynyrd	$17.99
00702182	The Essential Bob Marley	$16.99
00146081	Maroon 5	$14.99
00121925	Bruno Mars – Unorthodox Jukebox	$12.99
00702248	Paul McCartney — All the Best	$14.99
00125484	The Best of MercyMe	$12.99
00702209	Steve Miller Band — Young Hearts (Greatest Hits)	$12.95
00124167	Jason Mraz	$15.99
00702096	Best of Nirvana	$16.99
00702211	The Offspring — Greatest Hits	$17.99
00138026	One Direction	$17.99
00702030	Best of Roy Orbison	$17.99
00702144	Best of Ozzy Osbourne	$14.99
00702279	Tom Petty	$17.99
00102911	Pink Floyd	$17.99
00702139	Elvis Country Favorites	$19.99
00702293	The Very Best of Prince	$19.99
00699415	Best of Queen for Guitar	$16.99
00109279	Best of R.E.M.	$14.99
00702208	Red Hot Chili Peppers — Greatest Hits	$17.99
00198960	The Rolling Stones	$17.99
00174793	The Very Best of Santana	$16.99
00702196	Best of Bob Seger	$16.99
00146046	Ed Sheeran	$17.99

00702252	Frank Sinatra — Nothing But the Best	$12.99
00702010	Best of Rod Stewart	$17.99
00702049	Best of George Strait	$17.99
00702259	Taylor Swift for Easy Guitar	$15.99
00359800	Taylor Swift – Easy Guitar Anthology	$24.99
00702260	Taylor Swift — Fearless	$14.99
00139727	Taylor Swift — 1989	$19.99
00115960	Taylor Swift — Red	$16.99
00253667	Taylor Swift — Reputation	$17.99
00702290	Taylor Swift — Speak Now	$16.99
00232849	Chris Tomlin Collection – 2nd Edition	$14.99
00702226	Chris Tomlin — See the Morning	$12.95
00148643	Train	$14.99
00702427	U2 — 18 Singles	$19.99
00702108	Best of Stevie Ray Vaughan	$17.99
00279005	The Who	$14.99
00702123	Best of Hank Williams	$15.99
00194548	Best of John Williams	$14.99
00702228	Neil Young — Greatest Hits	$17.99
00119133	Neil Young — Harvest	$14.99

Prices, contents and availability subject to change without notice.

Visit Hal Leonard online at **halleonard.com**